SHAFTS OF SUNLIGHT

Also by Rita F. Snowden

SHAFTS OF SUNLIGHT

by

RITA F. SNOWDEN

HODDER AND STOUGHTON
LONDON AUCKLAND SYDNEY TORONTO

'I have seen these things in a shaft of sunlight.'

T. S. Eliot

To Rene

Preface

Always there is something special about 'firsts', though I cannot remember my first day on earth. Happily, that has not lessened what has followed.

I do remember my first 'shaft of sunlight' — from between trees it came across the short grass to meet me, and gladdened the shadows with meaning. And something like it has kept on happening ever since — a shadow, a mystery, a doubt, has received from beyond itself 'a shaft of sunlight', a lasting truth with freshness, to push out into age with undefeated youth at its heart. And here are some set down for sharing.

R.F.S.

Contents

I

An Essential Shaft

A leisurely meal with friends is likely to be an experience un-matched. When Dr. D. T. and Dulcie Niles were over from Ceylon, we fell to sharing discoveries. One story came uppermost; and without consciously planning it, we moved out of time into eternal dimensions.

Years before, when one of their sons — very small — got lost, they knew themselves all but distracted. At that point, Dulcie exclaimed: 'God is Love — nothing can happen to him!' But his father's reaction went deeper: '*Whatever happens*,' said he, '*God is still Love!*'

That is 'a shaft of sunlight' in any situation — *belief in the dependable character of God!* It was the assurance of our young Lord. Hanging stark on Golgotha, Death over-shadowing, He was able to say: 'Father, into Thy hands I commit my spirit!' He was Father, still — even there!

And I am at a loss to know how anyone can manage without an awareness of this kind of God, in this kind of world. Katherine Mansfield — our small country's story-teller — grew up amidst green things, the seasons rotating, sun, and at the day's end, moon and stars. Then she moved to Europe. And amidst the mountains of Switzerland, a day came when surrounded by the beauty and tonic-air of pine-forests, she found herself exclaiming: 'If only one could make some small grass-hoppery sound of praise to someone — thanks to someone, *but who*?'

André Gide admitted a like dilemma. In his *Journal* he wrote: 'Certain mornings are so gloriously pure that one doesn't know what to do with them. I would like to invent a God. So full is my heart of gratitude!' Growing up in the countryside — night and day, shadows and sunshine, the opening sentence of the Bible has satisfied me: '*In the beginning*

God created . . .' I have never been in a mood to accept as meaningful the jingle someone recited within my hearing:

> The earth's a lot of dust,
> The sky's a lot of air,
> The sea's a lot of water
> That *just happened* to be there!

A day came when I replaced it with four better lines from the poet Dryden, speaking of the world in which I found myself:

> This is a piece too fair
> To be the child of Chance, and not of Care:
> No Atoms casually together hurl'd
> Could e'er produce so beautiful a world!

Ernest, Lord Rutherford of Nelson — my relative — was the scientist who 'split the atom'. And when he returned, years later, to lecture where he grew up, I was proud to carry the entrance-ticket he gave me. Addressing men and women of science from all over the country, his words mostly went over my head; but one certainty I carried away — that even the atom, infinitesimal, could not be reckoned an accident of Chance. Behind its creation was a master-mind.

I had already read Huxley's defence of his claim to be 'agnostic' — from the inscription Paul the apostle had found in Athens: 'To the Unknown God.' 'God,' contended Huxley, 'was unknowable, because of His infinite nature, His absoluteness, His spirituality.'

But surely, to know this much about Him, was to know three tremendous truths; so He couldn't be altogether 'unknowable'. *'In the beginning God created the heavens and the earth!'* This essential truth a young member of Dr. A. J. Cronin's club sought — a little stammering fellow — when a visiting lecturer, atheistic, finished explaining how the pounding seas in prehistoric times beat upon the earth, till the result was a scum from which life emerged. At question-time, the little fellow found tongue to put his problem: 'Sir, you have explained how the b-big waves b-beat upon the shore, b-but

how did all that water get there in the first place?' Exactly!
Whether the Creator — as some contend — took six days of
the length we know them, or six million years, as some scien-
tists believe, leaves that opening statement of Scripture, un-
questioned. To this, I like to add words of my visiting friend,
Dr. D. T. Niles; 'This is God's world, and it is a world *which
He is creating*, not just a world that he has created.'

*   *   *

But one soon discovers one needs a fuller knowledge than
Nature alone can offer. When I first realised this, it was as
'a shaft of sunlight', lightening up much. I had till then, imagined that the poet Wordsworth found in Nature all that he
needed. Then I came across a letter of his to Sir George
Beaumont. Said he: '*I look abroad upon Nature*, and *I meditate
upon the Scriptures*, especially the Gospel of John, and my
creed rises up of itself, with the ease of an exaltation.' At the
heart of that lovely Gospel of John, which he favoured for his
spirit's aid, is the answer our Lord gave about God, when
questioned by one of His disciples: 'He that hath seen Me,'
said He, 'hath seen *the Father*' (John 14: 8–9). In other words:
'My inmost character, seen in Time, is what God is eternally.'

And in this more sophisticated age, I find Bishop Robinson
— author of the world-discussed book, *Honest to God*, at
pains to underline the very same thing, in terms of his own
experience: 'I do not pray,' says he, 'to "the Ground of my
being", I pray to *God the Father* ... to that utterly gracious
personal Reality which Jesus could only address as "Abba
Father!" I have no interest in a God conceived in vaguely
impersonal pantheistic terms.'

So I have come to feel when a golfing neighbour claims to
find on the links of a Sunday all that he needs to nourish his
spirit, or a fisherman friend argues for the silence of his
favourite stream, against the Gospels — including the Gospel
of John — and the sung hymns of the Church.

My friend, Professor Cecil Pawson passed on to me news of
his visit to the little church of Cossack, in the Galloway Hills.
There — in stained-glass and finely-worded plaque — he
saw anew the poet's splendid balance. Raised to Professor Clerk
Maxwell — first in Experimental Physics in the University

of Cambridge, whose theory later found consummation in the work of fellow-scientists pertaining to broadcasting and television — the tribute said: 'This window is erected by admirers of a genius that discovered the kinship between electricity and light, which led *through the mystery of Nature* to the fuller knowledge of God.'

But as my friend reminded me, Clerk Maxwell was already a man of Faith — bringing all he had to Nature — a worshipper, an elder in the Church, no less!

2

'Through Adam's Eyes'

It is a doubly happy thing when a church can be built amid Nature's beauty — that both may speak of God. In the sparsely-populated mountain area of New Zealand's West Coast, one such stands. And it has a wide window where in most churches, a tapestry hangs, so that a worshipper, facing the altar, looks out on to the *majesty* of God — the Franz Josef Glacier coming down between the mountains; and as foreground — on the altar of the church, the Cross, symbol of the *mercy* of God.

I set a picture of it in my devotional book: *While the Candle Burns* — which brought me a letter from an English bookseller. She had hoped — at first sight of it — that the little church was in the mountains in Switzerland; not half-a-world away, where she had small chance of ever visiting it. (I still look upon that picture as one of the most meaningful in my book.) And I count myself privileged that I have been several times able to sit in meditation in that little church in the mountains. A wonderful silence lays hold of one's spirit there.

From a local mountaineer, Alex Graham, I gleaned its story. 'About 1930,' he rejoiced to say, 'the Graham brothers

gave the land on which it stands. Reverend Jim Young was
then vicar; and he and Archdeacon Julian inspected the site,
and conceived the idea of placing the East window — an
inspired decision, that has made it world-known.

'After some time, Reverend A. K. Warren — later to be
Bishop Warren — took over. He actually helped us with the
"working-bee" that cleared space for the foundations,' said
Mr. Graham. 'This was originally covered with native forest.
He also superintended the erection of the building, and the
selection of its ecclesiastical fittings. The foundation-stone
was laid in time, by the Governor — dedication following
after an interval.

'Though built for eighty worshippers, a hundred and fifty
got in that memorable day. Of course, now,' he added, 'it's
open to any denomination, as well as for Anglican worship.
Mr. Mark Lyons served as our lay-reader for years — till the
war came, and he did not come back from Italy.'

*   *   *

Once, as I came away from that little church, my eyes lightened on a clump of fox-gloves, gracefully aspiring in a sunny
clearing nearby. They stood against great dark-green trees.

I had long loved fox-gloves — though as a child, neighbouring farmers had paid me honest coins to grub them up.
On my Saturday rambles, wherever I came across a bunch of
elliptical dull-green leaves, under-surfaces downy and paler
than the upper, there I was at liberty to grub. Once they
flowered, I found I could never do that.

When my friend Rene and I made our home at 'West Hills',
we cherished a few growing freely there. To confess as much,
even then, was to be ex-communicated from the company of
fastidious gardeners. Fox-gloves were weeds — the commonest
the purply-pink. Friend of breezes, they hung their long
pendulous flowers on one side of the stem, hairy and marked
with eye-like spots. 'Long-purples', the poet Tennyson called
them; another poet: 'The carillon of the wilds.' What those
otherwise kind neighbouring farmers, for whom I grubbed,
called them, need not be stated.

I did not then in the least guess that one day I would sing
praises to God for fox-gloves, for a medical reason. But that

day came — as I have told at length in my autobiography, *The Sun is High* — when I was smitten with a grievous heart-condition.

Much later — able to leave my bed and move about again — I made a visit to Britain; and whilst there, a pilgrimage to Birmingham, to Edgbaston Parish Church. This was meaningful to me, because there is the memorial to Dr. William Withering. (In my bag just then — and during many years — was a little bottle of brown pills — *digitalis*, a cardiac sedative, made from fox-gloves.) On the Doctor's memorial, before my eyes, was a beautifully fashioned fox-glove. The flower's curative properties had been first discovered — to the help of many of us — by the good Doctor.

I am thankful now, that nobody asks me — for small coins, or for prize-gardener's reasons — to grub up fox-gloves. Wherever I come across them, my heart rejoices!

* * *

Adam, I have understood since childhood, was the world's first gardener. His story I now know, belongs to the Childhood of the Race, when picture-language conveyed essential truth — pre-science Time. But however one now interprets the Garden-story, there is no questioning Julian Green's challenge: 'We need', says he, 'to see creation *through Adam's eyes* — to see everything for the first time, to look at a leaf as though one had never seen one before, for only then can it appear in all its newness!'

This power of one's early years so easily gets blunted — and more's the pity. '*God*,' as the apostle delighted to remind young Timothy, '*gives us richly all things to enjoy!*' (1 Timothy 6: 17). And it is through our senses that we enjoy these good things — the first sight and feel of hands and feet, the curved beauty of a loved-one's cheek, a dew-drop cradled in a leaf, a crocus pushing up into fresh, delicate life, the diamond-clear distance of the Pleiades — the seven little sister stars overhead.

One may live in a beautiful setting, and never see it, save when showing it to someone else — a child come for the holidays, with his Adam-tongue and eyes full of questions, or a friend freshly come from some other country.

And much the same must be said of the Bible, as of our

material, natural setting. We have known it so long, that some of its loveliest parts seem a little like well-tramped-on grass in a well-known picnic-ground. We have for some time given up coming to it with 'Adam's eyes'. It was a delight to meet in Professor T. E. Jessop's little book *Effective Religion*, the challenge I had heard him put: 'Has the Bible become dull to you? Naturally, if you haven't come to it on tip-toe, searching it with questions. Has worship lost its thrill? It is bound to do so if you come to it passively. Are you quickly at a loose end in prayer? Of course you are, if for you prayer means only telling God your wants, and if your wants are few. But the reading of the Bible and worship and prayer,' he adds joyously, 'should all be ways of exploring the immensity of God ... We cannot exhaust the inexhaustible.'

* * *

It was something of Adam's secret that later enabled a young shepherd in his setting on the back of the desert, to enter into a fresh experience, a new revelation of God. 'It may have been only a thorn bush that Moses saw that day,' as Francis B. James says, 'a thorn bush ablaze with blossom, or a tree in the flaming colours of Autumn, or the sun shining on a patch of vegetation, so that the man was awed and solemnised; he felt that he was on holy ground, and listened for what God had to say.' Then, jumping the centuries, as we must if others' early discoveries are to touch our lives at all, he finishes: 'Let me expect such moments for myself. God is always near. He has many ways of breaking in upon my life.'

I have just had an experience of this:

Rich,
    This morning opened for me full of miracle —
the breath of a Jersey cow with a coat of velvet,
lying lethargic, chewing her cud in the lane
by the hawthorn — a web cunningly spun
between two twigs out-stretched,
supporting microscopic globes
set in silver by the world's earliest Artist.

Hushed,
    I stood there, drenched in beauty, as if Time

in the haste of man's ways, had no meaning for me.
As if the God of galaxies far out, and near-by
hawthorn, knew better than any what Life
was all about. A simple man learned it once,
on the back of Horeb's desert, turning from minding
sheep, to hush his heart before a burning bush.

[R.F.S.]

3

Books Eagerly Opened

Year by year, I would call a holiday to celebrate one of my
chief joys, if I could tie it to a date. One day I couldn't read —
and the next day I could. It was 'a shaft of sunlight'.

I know now how fortunate I was to be born at the right time.
Once, children had no books — only Chapbooks, which were
not books at all, only boards printed with alphabets, Scripture-
texts, or mottoes, peddled around the countryside by Chap-
men. Illiteracy shed its dark shadow. Among fortunate adults,
the sun of truth had risen, but for children, it had hardly as
yet been proclaimed.

Then Mr. John Newbery — bless his name — came upon
the scene — the first publisher of children's books in English.
(I cannot be sure of the title of my own first book: I was
cutting my teeth at the time, so it hasn't survived.) But lately,
an old lady for whom I did a small service gave me a little
book bearing the proud name 'Newbery' — and thereby
hangs a tale of light and joy. It's title reads — with some elab-
oration — '*The Adventures of a Bee*, who invites all his little
friends to sip his honey, and avoid his sting'. It is embellished
with 'cuts' — charming wood-cuts — the whole book no
larger than four inches by two and a half. It's price was
'Four-pence', plainly printed on it; and just above, the

publisher's name: 'London, Printed for F. Power (grandson to the late Mr. J. Newbery) and Co. No. 65. near the Bar, St. Paul's Churchyard, 1790.'

I should like to have known Mr. Newbery, that whimsical, eccentric worker-of-miracles, to whom I owe so much — as does every child today. (The Newbery Medal is still regularly awarded for the best child's book published within a stated period.)

Dear Mr. Newbery set up in business at the Sign of the Bible and Sun, in St. Paul's Churchyard in 1744. Later, his notice of children's books appeared in the *General Advertiser*. It was for parents and nannies. 'Given gratis, by J. Newbery, ["only paying one penny for the binding"]: Nurse Truelove's Christmas Box, or the Golden Plaything for little children, by which they may learn the letters as soon as they can speak, and know how to behave so as to make everybody love them, adorned with thirty cuts.'

He often addressed himself directly to his little readers, and when they visited him with their nannies, gave small presents — bells to boys, and pin-cushions to little girls. (It would have been nice to have been one among the visitors to that chuckly old man — though I can't claim I've ever had a passion for a pin-cushion!)

Mr. Newbery published *Mother Goose's Melody*, and *Goody-Two-Shoes* — famous titles — and other tiny volumes bound in 'flowery gilt', a gay paper imported from the Netherlands. Both titles earned him the unprofitable compliment of being pirated by printer-publishers all up and down the land, and in America. (There was no law of copyright then.)

Nobody, at this date, even knows who the authors of those best-sellers were. Mr. Newbery was friend and patron of Oliver Goldsmith, Samuel Johnson, and other men of the pen of his day. It has been suggested that Goldsmith actually wrote *Goody-Two-Shoes* — but nobody knows. In those days, it was considered an undignified occupation for a learned adult to write for children. When he did, he took some pains to write an apology in a preface; or he by-passed recognition by assuming a pen-name — as Lewis Carroll did in his day — covering his identity as the Reverend Charles Lutwidge

Dodgson, mathematician and author-lecturer at Christ Church, Oxford. *Alice in Wonderland* got countless readers, in spite of his dodge.

In time, early 'cuts' gave way to line-drawings, by way of illustration; and they, in turn, to colour-plates, which quickened childish imagination to the edge of rapture. A new day was gradually dawning, when a child wanted to walk as tall as his shadow in cobbled streets.

But there were some adults who raised their voices against this advance. Said one, Maria Heck, in 1821: 'It may be doubted whether habituating children to seek amusement, almost exclusively, in fictitious narrative has not a direct tendency to weaken the natural powers.' And another was every bit as suspicious of *Robinson Crusoe*, which, she feared, 'might lead to an early taste for a rambling life and a love of adventure'. *Well*! This same lady had her doubts about *Cinderella*. 'It is,' she claimed, 'perhaps the most exceptionable book that has ever been written for children. It paints some of the worst passions that can enter the human breast — envy, jealousy, vanity.' *Well!*

So the battle for good books for children was never easily waged. Some of an educational and moral kind — when available — were abysmally dull. There was Dr. Brewer's *Guide to Science* — which at first looked promising. It was the work of a Trinity Hall scholar, the book in its twenty-sixth edition by 1869. But by the time it got to me, I had my doubts about it. It was written in catechism form — question and answer. Q. read: 'What is heat?' and pat came the answer: 'That which produces the sensation of warmth.' True! But not very exciting — not when one was ten! And a further crack in the facade of wisdom followed: 'Q. What is light?' the answer was: 'The *unknown* cause of visibility.' So dear Dr. Brewer *didn't* know everything, after all; I was so afraid he was going to. How much did he know? Perhaps he was just an honest soul filling in a gap that few others realised was a gap. One of his later questions made me feel a little tender towards him. The Q. was: 'What would a fearful person do to be secure in a storm?' And pat came the answer: 'Draw his bedstead into the middle of the room, commit himself to the care of God, and go to bed!' *Well!* No wonder the prospect of a ball with Cinderella or an escape with Robinson Crusoe had appeal for high-spirited children!

Books have become more and more lively with every year — and I have been able to own more and more; and even to add some of my own stories. Don't ask me — as everybody does — how many thousands of those volumes I have sold. I would have to look up my Statements over years; and I am kin to the little girl who wrote from her heart:

Arithmetic is such a bore
  I cannot stand it any more;
But if you'll take my good advice,
  You'll find that reading's very nice!

*   *   *

After a distinguished overseas journal published my story of Mr. Newbery, I received a letter from a gentleman in England, busy on a bibliography of publications bearing the imprint of Mr. John Newbery. He wrote: 'I was glad to read in *The Christian Science Monitor* sent me by a friend — that you have a copy of *The Adventures of a Bee*, 1790. Take care of it. The only other copy known to me is in the great collection of children's books formed by Miss Elizabeth Ball of Indiana, now in course of transfer to the Pierpont Morgan Library. So you are lucky to have a copy.'

If 'lucky' is the right word, then I am!

The truth is, I am never at ease with the word 'lucky'. I was very surprised to find good William Tyndale using it in his famous Bible translation. Of my early hero, Joseph, he said: 'And the Lord was with Joseph, and he was *a luckie fellowe*' (Genesis 39: 2).

Did he mean that God made a favourite of him? It couldn't be. One of my cherished, most straightforward texts, in Moffatt's modern translation — Acts 10: 34 — says: '*God has no favourites.*'

Words change their content — centuries have rolled by since Tyndale sat at his desk, pondering the 'luck' of Joseph. The Revised Standard Version — popular in this day — uses the word 'successful' to introduce Joseph. Success I can admit; but I am uneasy here, as always, about 'luck', though the word is often in my ears. Someone I casually meet shares news of some old school-fellow, who is 'down on his luck'. Or of himself, he relates a spin of ill-health, finishing his tale with, 'Isn't it just my luck?' Or, a bowler I admire suffers a misjudgment, and somebody beside me, watching for the minutes I am there, cries: 'O bad luck!'

Curiously, it was once the custom for a man of Faith — in taking leave of another — to use the words: 'Good luck, in the name of the Lord!' But that day has long disappeared, together with Tyndale's description of Joseph. As a person of Faith, I no longer think in terms of 'luck' — I do not expect to be specially preserved from accidents, germs, or the hazards of this age — otherwise my Faith would be little short of an insurance-policy — it would pay me to be Christian. No! I live in God's world, as a member of God's world-family — receiving much unearned good, as well as unearned ill, because of being bound up with others in the bundle of Life.

The power to read I cannot but count unearned good!

* * *

Through the years, I have had a good deal to do with children's books; buying them — always an early test when a desired book could compete with sweets or toys when one fingered pocket-money; selling them; minding them in a children's library; and in my turn, writing them.

Bridging the old days, with these, when books offer all manner of delights, I inherited the task of dismantling a children's library. It had been established many years in a City Mission, by a well-meaning, pious old gentleman. But it had long been out of use — and no wonder. I hoped that we might use the space.

The old librarian — and from all accounts, he had been a real lover of children — had actually gone to the bother of reading every single volume on his shelves. Proof was in the heavy pencil-markings that could be seen — scoring out each offending word he found: 'damn', 'curse', 'sneer', and the like. One or two of his 'old boys' to whom I reported my find, with some mirth — married men with children — related how they used to hold up the pages, one by one to the light, to read what was beneath the pencil-marks.

One other unexpected find I made was that whilst offending words could be dealt with, no attempt was made to deal with tear-jerking death-bed scenes, so common in those old volumes. Then I remembered that Death was a common 'visitor' among children, until this century; and as a result, a subject of instruction in youthful piety. (Even I could remember such stories that brought tears, as I sat on the bottom step of the stairs at Gran's house.) Head-stones in an old graveyard bore many children's names, and a proper Sunday afternoon's walk, in early times, had been to the nearest grave-yard to lay a bunch of flowers at the base of a weathering stone.

Some objected, but I think they must have been few: one of Lady Glenconner's children said: 'I think it is the name that is so frightening. I don't like to say it: it is so terrible, *Death*. I wish it wasn't *called* that! I don't think I should mind so much if it were called "Hig".'

So far we have now come that in 1954, a friend at Bexhill-on-Sea, told me that the word 'Cemetery' was banned from their bus time-tables and destination-boards, because of complaints that this was not 'a good advertisement for a health-resort'. *Well!*

Noel Coward in his play, *This Happy Breed*, shows us Frank and his sister in argument on this very issue. She uses a common term of evasion, concerning one — 'passed on'. Frank winces, and rebukes her: 'Mother died, see! First of all she got flu, and that turned to pneumonia, and the strain of that affected her heart, which was none too strong at the best of times, and she died . . . she didn't pass on, or pass over, or pass out — *she died*!'

Abrupt, perhaps; but in these days, a healthy swing of the pendulum. When so many are sacrificed in war; in violence; and on our roads; not to speak of sickness, and natural disasters, fires, floods, avalanches, earthquakes; it is foolish to pretend to evade Death's reality, by veering from mention of it.

Happily, handling children, as well as adults, a person of Christian Faith has deep and triumphant support.

4

Green Company

I rejoice continually in the company of trees and water. Half-an-hour taken from work this morning gave me this word-picture:

> This is a generous day,
>   when each brown duck swims double,
> each pine punctures the sky
>   and pierces the lake's heart,
> as I meander by.
> Here, a child in a red coat
>   near the edge,
> has a play-mate in a red coat, pellucid,
> where the elements earth, air and water
>   peacefully float.   [R.F.S.]

*   *   *

Should a day ever come when I must choose between flowers and trees, I know what my choice will be — though I hope that day never comes. Trees have such a companionable nature; know such diverse moods. If it is relaxation I need, they are a strong support; if I am sad of heart, they seem to share my lot unobtrusively; if I am gay, they respond, as to light winds, adding frolicksome fun. The pungency of pine-needles beneath parent trees is enough to recall nights out-of-doors in my sleeping-bag. With stars overhead, the hours then mark changes in the face of Nature.

The word 'tree', H. L. Edlin says, 'is derived from the Anglo-Saxon *treow*. Trees', he declares, 'have been known to man since the days before his speech began.' I do not remember when first I came to love trees — it may have been before my speech began.

From the beginning, kinsfolk have fashioned houses, and raised places of worship; sailed the wide seas in wooden vessels; and in their domestic life, found a score of uses for bark, stain and gum. Without trees — receiving rain, and filtering it to the earth, through the leafy floor, there could have been no fertility; no roots holding together farms, roads and hilly gardens against erosion and loss. Not to mention the year-round effect on the weather.

On a journey I made lately — exchanging the pressures of the city for the patient growth of the countryside — I came upon a notice in large letters beside a stand of pines: 'FIRE DANGER. MATCHES HAVE HEADS BUT NO BRAINS! BE CAREFUL!' In that, I was reminded of how greatly trees suffer at our hands. Too few of us seem to have come across that word of Scripture, which says: '*Hurt not the earth . . . nor the trees!*' (Revelation 7: 3) This has long been one of my favourite texts. Unfortunately there are many ways of 'hurting trees'. Fire, is only one — though the notice-board I happened on, was repeated at intervals all through that green forest area.

Research in recent times, has shown us the tragedy of foolish felling. The Sahara itself was not always the desert it is now. Successive generations of nomadic men ignorantly felled its virgin forests, leaving in their tracks an arid desolation. Parts of Africa, once densely populated, have become grave-yards of vanishing peoples, directly as the outcome of widespread destruction. The great prairies have had their trees up-rooted, felled and stripped; and other parts of the earth's surface, once clad in living green, have been turned into dust-bowls. In China, over generations, the Yellow River — year by year — has swirled away to the sea tons of soil. And even in the new lands that some of us know best, the story of erosion is a painful one.

A more modern 'hurt' is the hungry need for newsprint. We must have it, of course — but there is need for restraint, and for replanting. In the States — I learned when I was there — one Sunday edition of a metropolitan newspaper uses up twenty-four acres of forest! *Imagine it !* An ordinary Chicago daily uses a hundred acres each week! Turning over some of those 'jumbo' papers, not to mention some of the magazines on the news-stands with trashy contents, I have been obliged to agree with my good friend Teresa Hooley:

How many trees have died,
In all their loveliness and pride —
Home of a myriad wings,
Articulate with wind-taught utterings,
Or tranced in rain-quiet summer eves;
How many trees
For these few worthless leaves ?'

We have an obligation, surely, to look into the future,
beyond our own brief span. Old Dr. Robert Thomas Cooper
used to divide people up into two. 'There are only two kinds
of people in the world,' said he, 'the good and the bad. The
division is very simple — *the good people plant trees, the bad*
cut them down.' Tree-lover though I am, I think that is an
over-simplification, but certainly it takes more forethought
to plant and nourish, than to destroy.

When I wrote in a British paper, in this mood, one apprecia-
tive reader addressed me, through the Editor: 'I wonder if Miss
Snowden knows of the "Plant a Tree" effort by the A.A.?
Motorists here have been asked to send a pound, and say where
they'd like their tree planted (a list of counties given.) Later,
we heard when and where this would take place. On 1st and
2nd November, Forestry experts planted trees in thirty-four
different counties — altogether twelve thousand young trees,
sweet chestnut, red oak, white poplar, oak, lime, elm, horse
chestnut, rowan, wild cherry, field maple, Norway maple,
sycamore, white willow and beech . . . It was rightly said to be
"the biggest army ever mobilised in the name of rural herit-
age."'

Lately, my love of trees gave me this poem, which I titled:
'Tall Against the Sky:'

A tree trusts to no calendar, only the seasons'
          sap,
to no alarm-clock, sleeping late, rising
          early,
its obedience to life is a grace no man
          knows;
tender in Spring's green, adventurous in
          Summer,

Autumn's felicities clothed in generous
      gold,
Winter's spare gift filigreed against the
      sky.

Who can remember his first tree — looked-up-into,
      loved?
Rocks covet only a shallow covering of
      lichen,
but a tree spells out clearly the Creator's
      purpose —
a ministry in scent and shade, strength and
      usefulness,
rain trickling into the thirsty earth
      waiting,
fields, gardens, hills saved from aridity and
      erosion,
with a family house raised from strong-grained
      timber.

He who plants a tree, lends his slight aid to God's
      purpose,
a wonder each season renewed for those who look
      on it,
he plants a friend of sun, wind and
      sky,
a shaft of shimmering beauty towering
      high,
a kindness for creatures, as for his fellow-
      men,
he incarnates a green thought born with the birth
      of Time,
and on-going generations will bless
      him.   [R.F.S.]

5

Experience Shared

Nobody ever told me, when first I opened the prized Family Bible, that I couldn't read it like any other book. Naturally, I began at the beginning. And soon — despite my eager joy in most reading — I got bogged down in the pages of Leviticus. It now seems a wonder that I got that far; perhaps it was that I'd been told many of the stories I came across in Genesis and Exodus. But Leviticus proved hopeless.

There my Bible-reading might have stopped forever — save that a year or two later, I learned that the Bible wasn't a book at all. *It was a library of books!* This was a veritable 'shaft of sunlight' to me — and in my 'teens, I began again. (Of course, I'd never heard of anybody reading a library of books straight through. No wonder I couldn't get far with my approach.) Soon, I learned another thing — *the Bible wasn't written by God*, or by any one of His servants to a mechanical order: 'Isaiah, take down a prophecy, please!' It was written by people, with human differences, living in varying circumstances, over as long as fifteen hundred years! 'The Bible,' as Elton Trueblood says neatly, 'is a record of God's unique dealings with men, but it is not, for the most part, a book about good men.'

More than that, it is written in various types of literature — in history, poetry, visions, old-world story, prayer, parable, drama, letter, etc. So one must read accordingly.

Then, too, one has to regard the on-going progression of religious ideas therein — the Old Testament first, then the New. Some of its earliest parts are as simple as childhood stories — the thoughts of Abraham, and others of my heroes. Even the prophets, well on in time, have each to lay hold of a fuller idea of God, as time passes. Isaiah thinks of Him as a God of *Holiness*; Amos as a God of *Judgment*; Hosea, in his turn, as all these, but above all, as a *God of Mercy*! Line by line the picture is filled in, till men hear Jesus saying that God is supremely a *God of Love*. And this is elaborated in the New Testament. It would have been unwise to have given this full revelation all at once — men and women weren't ready for it.

In exactly the same way, *the moral values of the Bible are seen to rise*. In the early parts there are bloody massacres credited to God; even in the Psalms, where there are lovely songs, consoling passages about the Shepherd, and assurances about being kept day and night, there are passions and purposes revolting in our ears. We are free to skip such passages in public and private devotions, but we are bound to admit they're in the Book. Painfully, one meets in Psalm 137: 'O daughter of Babylon . . . happy shall he be that rewardeth thee as thou hast served us. Happy shall he be that taketh and dasheth thy little ones against the stones.' In another instance: 'Joshua never withdrew the hand that held his javelin until he had massacred all the people of Ai, both men and women, even as the Lord God had commanded him.' And there is the story of Agag, a helpless old man, savagely hacked to pieces by Samuel. There is the account of Jepthah vowing before God that if only He will deliver the people of Ammon into his hands, he will sacrifice to His name the first living thing that comes to meet him on his return. He *is* victorious; but the first to meet him is none other than his only daughter. And he takes her life — both persuaded that the God with whom they are called to deal, is the kind of God who will be pleased by this senseless sacrifice. It's a long way short of the sublime passages of tender love, in the New Testament. That there is so much in the Old, of which Christian conscience disapproves, only proves that men had to move upward step by step. So it follows that where light is sought for modern-day behaviour and religious truth, the New Testament supersedes the Old every time, whenever the two passages one might quote, appear to clash.

Why then, some will ask — and it seems at first sight, a reasonable request — bother about the Old Testament at all?

To answer with the obvious, the *New grows out of the Old* — and the New Testament writers are intensely aware of this, and refer to it continually. Jesus had only the Old Testament — and spoke of fulfilling it, not ignoring it. 'We need the Old

Testament, that we may understand the New — to show the
pit out of which humanity has been dug,' we can say to those
who deprecate the Old Testament being read at all today. The
fascinating stories of persons, and nations, their aspirations,
their acts of courage, are of immeasurable value. In the pages of
Job, the Psalms, and Prophets there is much of value to the
growth of the race, that does not appear in the New Testament.

This Book deals with men and women with passions like
our own, inextricably mixed in the business of living, as no
other does. And where is a book so honest? Whilst it never
falters in its witness to God and His on-going purpose in the
affairs of the nations, it never fails to record moral lapses on the
part of its heroes, and never condones them. We are introduced to David the 'comely youth', the 'sweet singer', but we
meet him also as the cad who sends a gallant captain to his
death, because he wishes to seduce his charming wife; Joshua
leads his people courageously, but he also loses his temper
when a handful of children poke fun at him. Even in this day,
we can welcome literature that offers such honesty. Not that
one must think of the Bible — Old Testament, or New —
as above all, literature. It's not. C. S. Lewis sets this down
plainly, for those content to prate about the Bible being 'the
monument of English prose': 'Those who read the Bible as
literature,' said he, 'do not read the Bible.'

Above all else, it is a sacred book, a religious book, telling
of the experience of men and women with God. It is not to be
a task enjoined; the reading of it is to enrich us, and delight
us. How much poorer our ordinary conversation would be —
to say no more — without its choice references to 'the strength
of the hills', 'a thorn in the flesh', 'hoping against hope',
'treasures of the snow', 'honour to whom honour is due',
'mine own familiar friend', 'those who go down to the sea in
ships', 'riotous living', 'filthy lucre', 'in the twinkling of an eye',
'the powers that be', 'still waters'.

Some time ago the British and Foreign Bible Society had a
stall showing Bibles in various bindings — red, green, blue, as
well as black. And one woman passing noticed them, and picked
up one with the question: 'Is there anything fresh in it?'

There is always something fresh in the Bible for anyone of
who approaches it intelligently, bearing in mind these points

and preserving a humble eagerness. Without the Old Testament record of the long stumbling way by which men and women have come — each experience adding something of significant truth hitherto unguessed — it is impossible to fully appreciate and love the New Testament as we now have it.

6

Many Miracles

I am a reasonable gardener — having started with my father and mother, who were great gardeners. But I have never been able to garden in Latin — each year I learn some new names, and each year forget. I don't know why it is — I have a good memory for most things — still the fact remains.

But one doesn't need Latin to enjoy a garden. At 'West Hills', Rene and I gardened two-fifths of an acre. We have less now that we live on the North Shore, so that the battle with weeds, birds and blights is less demanding; though, of course, it remains — that's part of gardening. A delightful old record from Tudor times tells how the 'weeding women' at Hampton Court were paid 2d to 3d a day, with free meals of bread, herrings and 'other things washed down with ale', to keep the weeds in check. They were provided with stout leather gloves, iron-tipped, to root out 'unprofitable herbs'.

The first gardening book ever written for women, was written by a man, William Lawson, in 1618. That's a long time ago. In it he urged that the mistress herself should be present when gardening was in progress, 'to teach her maids to know herbs from weeds'. Very sensible; but we modest gardeners of modern times, have to teach ourselves. The curious thing, of course, is that weeds in one country, can be choice flowers in another. Some while ago, the women of Pasadena held the world's first weed-show; and it was an unqualified success. Many weeds have long seemed to me attractive — but if one is to garden, out they must come.

And there are winged and legged pests. I've long had a kinship with the politician-poet of our day, A. P. Herbert, since he wrote two unforgettable lines:

Greenfly, it's difficult to see
Why God, who made the rose, made thee.

Encouraged to find relief in rhyming, I lately wrote 'A Letter in Reply' — addressed to one, *Dear Snail*:

You came before my usual morning mail
and left a letter on my doorstep,
scrawled in silver ink, as always,
to tell me that my lettuces were gone —
my baby ones, pride of my heart;
and now I am bereft.

You hadn't need to write —
I'd have known in time. I've had a screed
from you before — in the same scrawl,
in the same ink. Don't write again
unless you have some better news —
just now I am bereft. [R.F.S.]

But despite all, gardeners press on, because we know that there is nowhere else such pleasure to be found. I have a tender love for Diocletian, because of his response to the urgent message which reached him from Rome in the early days, asking him to return, and to 'put on purple', and all the responsibilities that went with it. He replied that if only Maximilian could see the cabbages which he had raised with his own hands, he would never urge him to relinquish the joys of life, for the pursuit of power. And that sense of values remains among many of us. We understand Bacon's meaning when he said: 'God Almightie first planted a Garden, and indeed, it is the Purest of Humane Pleasures.' Stretching across the centuries, H. J. Massingham of our day speaks for many beside himself: 'Lightheartedly enough, I began my career as a gardener ... It is my deliberate conviction, after forcing my way through thickets of error and labyrinths of follies, that the good gardener is one of the world's elect, beside whom the statesman, the philosopher, and even the physicist are comparatively small beer ... To make a good gardener requires not one but ten life-times, so infinite is the knowledge, beautifully balanced the tact and skill.'

Miss Kingsley wrote in praise of her garden: 'Unlike other works of art, there is no finality in a garden. The picture once painted, the statue once sculptured, it is finished. But the garden goes on growing as long as time and love of it shall last, each succeeding year adding some fresh touch ... fresh surprises.' Many a time in our own little garden, I come upon a miracle — see it with my own eyes. Out of our unexceptional soil, with what effort we are able to make, comes such beauty of colour, such shape, and perfume! If such a thing happened once, we would proclaim it to the entire countryside; but because it happens season by season, we are in danger of taking it for granted.

Elizabeth Goudge, in our day, speaks of old Bates the gardener. Asked whether he believed in God or not, he replied: 'Yes, sir, I took religion when I started gardening. Wot I say is 'oo put them peas in them pods, an' made them flowers so pretty an' all?'

Miracle lies at hand daily, for all those of us who love gardens — all depends on whether we have open eyes to see how near it is! Of course, those who are not able to see miracles in the garden, are not likely to see them in the Gospels.

*   *   *

To ask, with Dr. Harry Fosdick: 'What exactly is a miracle?' is to find a definition as simple, and yet awe-inspiring. '*A miracle is God's use of His law-abiding powers to work out — in ways surprising to us — His will for our lives and for our world.*' *Miracles are not magic* — I remember the first time this dawned upon me, as 'a shaft of sunlight'. Two pieces of slender stick — crossed by a small boy, and covered with calico — make up an object heavier than air, that tossed up, will fall to the ground. The law of gravity sees to that. But there are also laws of wind-pressure; and a small boy's kite can be seen to fly — though he may not know why, and count it a miracle. Miracles do not demand interference with natural laws — only the working-out of other laws of which we know little or nothing, sometimes combining a number.

It doesn't follow that Jesus — in healing the sick, and crippled — interfered with law. Why should He? It wasn't necessary. He obeyed laws and used laws unknown to most at the time — indeed, unknown to some of us still. Someone has said: 'The miracles of Jesus were the ordinary works of His Father, wrought small and swift.' But He was very careful when, and where He worked them — anxious always not to 'brow-beat' the minds of men. When He did do a miracle on an over-whelming scale — as when He matched the need of the moment, by feeding the five thousand with a few loaves and fishes — He straightway sought to escape from them. They wanted to make Him King; and He would not have His kingship dependent on miracles. He wanted to be received for Himself — for His quality of spirit. His truth revealed, His lasting revelation of God.

Jesus' miracles, as recorded in the Gospels, were not short-cuts, and never performed for His own comfort or convenience; always they were for the glory of God, the Father. Had He cared, He could have saved Himself the harshness and humiliation of the Trial, and death of on the Cross. He admitted as much: 'Think ye not that my Father could provide Me with a company of angels?' He had only to ask.

One is also struck by this fact — against the grotesque 'miracles' recorded in the Apocryphal gospels, the miracles of Jesus stand out clearly in purpose, compassion and dignity.

If you ask me which I count the greatest, I still think, with Dr. Micklem, the turning of Peter the undisciplined fisherman, into Peter the Apostle; the turning of street-stained Mary Magdalene into the loving, gracious woman of the first Easter days; the turning of fear-filled followers, into men of incomparable courage! Dr. Micklem puts it simply: 'The greatest miracle recorded of Jesus of Nazareth is that He made Simon the Zealot and Matthew the publican sit down together at the same table like brothers and friends.' True! And He goes on performing miracles of this kind — and I never cease to marvel at them!

7

'Love, Honour and . . .'

I've just been to a wedding!

At weddings round the world and back again, I've listened to bride after bride vow to 'love, honour and obey'. Of late, the word 'obey' has been dropped out. Now another change has occurred — and a good one, surely; the bride has undertaken to 'love, honour — *and forgive!*'

This touches married bliss, and home-making at its deepest level. In the Lord's Prayer, the petition for bread is followed immediately by the petition: '*Forgive us . . . as we forgive.*' And how right the link is; for what is bread — in marriage, or out of it — if for any reason, one's spirit is estranged? This is something deeper than to forget. Every one of us — in marriage, and out of it — needs to hold close to our hearts, the poet's beautiful statement:

'Tis sweet to stammer one letter
of the Eternal's language, on earth
it is called *forgiveness.*

Whenever we take upon our lips the petition of The Lord's Prayer, 'Forgive us . . . as we forgive', we acknowledge ourselves part of God's world-family, stating a basic need. Every night, before she surrendered herself for sleep, Ellen Terry set herself to forgive any with whom she had been at cross-purposes during the day. 'One must do so', she reasoned, 'else how is it possible to repeat The Lord's Prayer?' Exactly! 'We love Him because He first loved us' — God, in this way, takes the initiative; but love and forgiveness are inseparable. We cannot have a happy marriage, family home, short of this reality day by day. We are human beings. 'To forgive, is to say to one who has done wrong — and to have it true: "I do not think of you or feel toward you as one who has done this; I do not hold it in my heart against you; I leave it out of my thoughts so that it does not embarrass the relationship between you and me; it is between us as if it had not been!" ' (*Outline of Christian Theology* by W. N. Clark, D.D.) But though we absorb this text-book definition, in our fractured relationships, in the most real way, *there are still some things that forgiveness cannot do.* I remember well when this first dawned upon me.

The actual deeds of the past performed by the one now forgiven, still exist — they have become part of human-history. Nothing can wipe them out. In this sense, there is truth in Omar Khayyam's words, that I have never really liked:

The Moving Finger writes; and having writ
Moves on: nor all your Piety nor Wit
Shall lure it back to cancel half a line,
Nor all your Tears wash out a Word of it.

And the natural consequences of the deeds done, remain — the spoiling of bodily fitness, through dissipation, or ignorance, is not instantly mended by forgiveness, if ever — more than that, the sorrowful consequences bear down on one's family and friends.

Nor does forgiveness instantly and mysteriously remove one's disposition to sin. One may forgive another's irresponsibility with drink, with cash, with sex, with gossip; but there is in forgiveness no guarantee that these human tragedies will never recur.

And though the other whom one has forgiven is grateful for it, the remembrance of the past wrong-doing remains. When a father forgives a son, it does not follow that either shall forget that wrong has been done; but it does determine how the father will feel and react, and that memory for both of them, will not be soured.

Forgiveness is not a light-hearted matter — whether between our Eternal Father and ourselves one by one, as members of His world-family, or as individuals in family-life, community, or national-life. We cannot accept Heine's saying on his death-bed: 'God will forgive me, 'tis His trade.' And the attitude of Westcott's character who drawled out the following words is as false: 'Wa'al, if I've done anything I'm sorry for, I'm willin' to be forgi'n.' Forgiveness is costly, always — whether it is the forgiveness of a sinful child by the Eternal Father, or the forgiveness of one by another of us in a close human family-relationship.

What can forgiveness do, then? It can bridge over strained relationships — so the sooner forgiveness is offered the better; there is no need, like Ellen Terry, to wait till the end of the day — though it would be foolish to wait longer. Forgiveness can also cancel the guilt of sin, and prepare for a new and better day. And these two discoveries are unspeakably precious, one finds.

It is estimated that the Lord's Prayer, with that telling, two-fold petition: *'Forgive us . . . as we forgive'*, now rises from earth in twelve-thousand different languages. We cannot pray this prayer whilst we hold grudges, and nurse hatred and bitter feelings toward any. Forgiveness means much more than a penalty remitted: it means a relationship restored. When we each pray the familiar words: *'Forgive us, as we forgive'*, we really mean, 'Father, grant to me that degree of forgiveness that I am willing to extend to people who are out of harmony with me — people I don't like, people who do stupid and hurtful things.' There is no forgetting the old saint, George Herbert's words: 'He who cannot forgive breaks the bridge over which he himself must pass.'

I am not now surprised, as when Muriel Lester said to me: 'I'm afraid of the Lord's Prayer.' We sat together talking on a Y.W.C.A. balcony made available to us. Forgiveness can never be counted a weakness, at best a 'churchy sentiment' — it is one of the great essentials of this life at every level, and relationships cannot go on without it. Through a Swiss Red-Cross worker, I heard of a poor, wretched Greek woman. 'Last month,' she said, 'I had three children, but there wasn't enough food to go round, so I had to let my daughters die.' 'How did you decide which of the children to keep?' asked the worker. 'Oh!' she replied, 'I had to keep my son so that he could revenge his sisters.' Such an attitude cannot serve life; a new world cannot be born in such a spirit. It calls for a healed relationship — *and that is the one great thing that Forgiveness does*. It's a *family experience*. 'If ye forgive men their trespasses', that great Prayer emphasis goes on, 'your heavenly Father will also forgive you: but if ye forgive not ... neither will your Father forgive your trespasses.' (Matthew 6: 14–15). The family obligation of forgiveness — God's heavenly forgiveness and our earthly forgiveness are now for ever joined, and no man can put them asunder. Clearly, our readiness to forgive cannot be the *cause* of the Father's forgiveness — but it is the *condition* on which it becomes effective. Hearts that harbour revenge, fault-finding, or even indifference, are in no fit state to receive the forgiveness of the Father, or the forgiveness of a fellow-human.

Forgiveness has its birth in genuine Love — and is the wonder of being trusted again within the family. So there can hardly be a better vow for any one of us to take, than 'to love, cherish — *and forgive !*'

8

All Our Senses

The pungent scent of a bonfire is drifting in at my open window. And it's lovely. Somebody is tidying up his gathered leaves and hedge-cuttings. In the petrol-cursed atmosphere of most of our cities, something desperate is happening to our senses. And we are losing some of God's gifts to us.

Of course, our senses have always been less than those of wild creatures — we've never been able to smell like a dog, hear like a deer, or feel electrical influences like migrating birds. But our senses matter supremely, nevertheless. (It may be that they differ in *kind* from those possessed by the creatures, so that a dog's sense of smell may be related acutely only to animal smells, and food, and have no meaning in relation to a flowering clover-field, or a hedge garlanded with honeysuckle.)

In childhood, senses are very acute — though not fully developed. Ruth Ainsworth speaks of them, very charmingly. Of children, she says:

Each morning brings a world of their own making,
    with colours scarcely dry,
created at the moment of awaking,
    by ear and hand and eye.

Childhood's powers are not spoiled by sophistication — by highly-spiced foods, speed, or petrol-fumes. I often think of the tragedy that befell Helen Keller, as a child, when early smitten blind and deaf. In time — to the surprise of the whole world — she managed to achieve great powers of responsiveness. Before I had the privilege of meeting her, and hearing her lecture to a university gathering that hung on her every word, toilfully expressed, I had been impressed by what she had passed on about the senses. 'I who am stricken blind,' she dared to say, 'can give but one hint to those who see. One admonition to those who would make full use of the gift of sight. Use your eyes as if you would be stricken blind. And the same method could be applied to other senses. *Make the most of every sense.*' And above any other, who has risen to a life of rich service, I knew she had the right to offer such words.

But as well, those of us greatly enriched by our senses ought to hear C. S. Lewis, in our day, as he tellingly underlines what he calls 'the stewardship of the senses'. It is a good reminder of our responsibility.

Among our five senses, dominant is the sense of sight. Most of us value this, and immediately seek help at the first hint of trouble. Sylvia Townsend Warner extends the challenge further. She has watched many travellers about England. 'For every hundred who travel with eyes,' she says, 'there are perhaps thirty who travel with ears, and remember among the events of a journey, the ring of a forge, the mock-turtle sobs of a draining-pump, the Sunday burst of hymnody from church or chapel.'

'We poor mortals live in our *five senses*', Luther liked to say. But of some of us, it doesn't seem wholly true — we exercise but part of them. Paul's words to young Timothy could well become a text we should cherish: '*God . . . giveth us richly all things to enjoy*' (1 Timothy 6: 17). And we are one by one, answerable for such delights. I once heard these words misread in a public-place: 'God . . . giveth us richly all things to *endure*.' But it's not 'endure', it's 'enjoy', and we cannot respond fully, unless we do 'live in our *five senses*'.

*   *   *

To get away into the freshness of the unspoiled country, has been several times my lot. One memorable week under the blue of a summer's sky, I kept company with our country's longest river — the Waikato — moving down two hundred green satin miles to the sea. At no point did it weary on the way — nor did we. I couldn't have had a better companion than my friend Harold. He possessed an old car, just right to carry our gear to our meeting-place with the River; and most important of all, he possessed eagerness, and a good pair of feet.

The very hour his note of acceptance arrived, I sorted out my stout shoes, trusty haversack, a piece of canvas, and camping-gear; and from a store hired two sleeping-bags. I railed them to Harold's family-home, deep in the country.

Well packed, the old car brought us next day by a winding road to our first night's pitch — a disused gravel-pit. Nearby, trickled the infant river.

That evening — and it was a beautiful one, with high billowing clouds — Harold tied the piece of canvas to the hood of his old car, and fastened its extreme edge to the earth. Then we gathered up armfuls of dry tussock to give a little comfort beneath our sleeping-bags. 'Look! Up there, is kapok in plenty!' exclaimed my companion, 'and we sleep on this!' Our camp at last in order, we laid plans to walk up on to the breast of the mountain nearest, on the morrow, to the birth-place of the river. (I had searched in vain, in every book-shop and library, to find a book on it. It seemed, perhaps, that this was the next book I should myself write.)

Night descended — calm and all embracing. My mind flew to Robert Louis Stevenson's words about night spent out-of-doors: 'Night is a dead monotonous period under a roof; but in the open world, it passes lightly, with its stars, dews and perfumes, and the hours are marked by changes in the face of Nature.' My senses were responsive, though I hadn't managed as well as R.L.S. to wiggle out a little hollow for my hip. By the time I managed it, morning had all but come.

Harold lost no time in kindling a fire to serve us, under shelter of a sandy bank, and setting the billy on it. In turn, I started to cook the camp-breakfast — on the up-turned billy lid over the boiling water, bacon-and-eggs — supported with crisp, golden toast speared on the sharp end of a stick, the billy offering water for tea. Golden marmalade came out of a tin.

Before the promising heat of the day could make things trying, we started out hopefully. Hour after hour pushed us on. We met no one; save for a couple of birds overhead, we saw no creature. As the mood dictated, we crossed over from one bank to the other — the river lessening in width as we walked.

In time, we came to the actual birth-place — a small, clear pebbly pool, on the third of the mountains which made up the grandeur of National Park — given to the people of New Zealand by the Maori Chief, Te Heuheu. 'If we had come all this way,' said my friend, 'to find this mighty River starting in a marshy, boggy ooze, I'd have been sadly disappointed. *But this is decent!*' and repeating his words, he walked round that pool, '*This is decent!*' Then he took a photograph of one of my stout tramping-shoes *bridging it!* I was intrigued that at any part of the glorious river I could bridge it at will.

A few minutes' rest was welcome. Then we turned, to keep the ever-widening river company on its way down. Several streams contributed a little. Soon, it was too wide to jump from side to side; and by mid-afternoon, we were back at our gravel-pit camp-site. It had been a hot, but rewarding tramp. Our week-long acquaintance with the river had begun well.

A second night passed beneath the stars, there, before we were on our way a few miles downstream in the old car. We came to a trout-hatchery; and then to a point beloved of trout-fishermen — in rapids and pools — and in time to the shore of our country's largest lake, Taupo, wherein, for a time, the river surrendered its identity.

There, we visited a Maori *pa* — a long-established village on the Lake's bank — and paid a visit to Hepi Te Heuheu, Paramount Chief of the Ngati-Tuwharetoa tribe. (He was, as we expected, English-speaking, though the fact that Harold could speak Maori helped to establish our welcome.) Presently, we were reverently led to the last resting-place of his distinguished ancestor. (Legend has it that *his* ancestor had 'lighted the fires in the mouth of volcano, Ngauruhoe', one of the three great mountains.) It was impressive to be so received; in my Raetihi mission-days, I had lived within sight of the National Park — snowy heights, tree-clad slopes, distant, but ever changing in mood.

The next few days we spent around the attractive lake's rim — rejoicing in its shimmering beauty, twenty-five miles long, by eighteen-and-three-quarters wide, our map claimed.

Fishing-camps were here and there. For two nights, at the end of days of exploration, we forsook our sleeping-bags, for fishermen's bunks, and meals cooked for hungry appetites at day's end. Nearby, were natural hot-pools in which children bathed; others were boarded over and around for adults. A little further on, were delightful limestone caves — offering fantastic stalactites and stalagmites. From the lake's township, many set out in boats of various kinds; and here and there, one came upon more elaborate accommodation for tourists. It was good to take advantage of one of these.

Then came another sleeping-place under the stars. This time, we set up camp beneath a stand of ancient pine-trees — and taking the place of the tussock, chosen early on, to soften our slumbers were pungent pine-needles. And Nature couldn't have made us a kinder gift. The hills, silhouetted against the evening sky, supported young pine-forests; near at hand, the river — limpid and wide now — slipped by, rainbow-trout there, plopping and plopping as the mood took them.

On and on, we kept the river company when daylight came — as it ran past historic battle-sites, where Maori braves had matched traditional skills with those of English 'red-coats' in the early days of colonisation, when relationships were brash.

Further miles brought wide green farm-lands, with roads multiplied, and kindly bridges. We came to the tree-blessed town of Cambridge; and Hamilton next, boasting of city status.

Still, the glorious river — ever widening — moved onwards

to the sea; still the sky overhead was blue, and our week out-of-doors full of reward; my senses registering the secret of life, *the river's receiving and giving !* No book resulted, but this was enough!

9

Mark's Little Book

The word 'marvellous' has never been one that I have much used; but it is marvellous to share thoughts and experiences with writers living afar, some in other ages. Their books make this possible — brought from the shop, the library, or a friend's shelves. The idea of reading a few sentences morning or evening, or contenting oneself with an incident out of context, would never occur — though curiously, many read in this manner 'One of the most marvellous little books in the world'. 'A shaft of sunlight' came into my life when first I read Mark's Gospel whole, at one sitting.

Matthew, Mark and Luke share one title: 'The Synoptic Gospels' — the word in the Greek, meaning 'to see together'. Each adds much; though I always now urge Mark as the best starting-place — and not only because a small boy I once taught, confessed that starting with Matthew, he 'got bogged in all *the beggots*'. It's opening verses are, of course, those favoured by Jewish readers, loving genealogies — recording how somebody 'begat' somebody, and somebody 'begat' somebody else. Apart from this obstacle, Mark actually came first in point of time. Added to this, it's a story full of action — with lovely words that appeal — 'immediately', 'straightway', 'forthwith', and 'a young man came running'.

'It would be possible,' underlines my friend Dr. William Barclay, with supporting scholarship, 'to urge that Mark's Gospel is *the most important book in the world.*' Certainly,

Anthony Bloom — our day's distinguished Archbishop of the Russian Orthodox Church in Britain — would support that. Whilst he was a student in Paris, Faith slipped from him. Then, under pressure, he went in a surly mood to a lecture on Christ and Christianity. The outcome had best be told in his own words: 'I hurried home,' said he, 'in order to check the truth of what the lecturer had been saying. I asked my mother whether she had a book of the Gospels ... I expected nothing good from the reading, so I counted the chapters of the four gospels to be sure that I read the shortest, not to waste time unnecessarily. And thus it was *the Gospel according to St. Mark* which I began to read.

'I do not know how to tell what happened ... Before I reached the third chapter, I was aware of a Presence. I saw nothing, I heard nothing. It was no hallucination. It was a simple certainty that the Lord was standing there, and that I was in the presence of Him.'

What other small book anywhere, I wonder, could do that for such a reader, in such a short time, and so lastingly? (The pity is, that for so many, addicted to a few verses at a time, it never gets a chance.)

Without doubt, Mark's Gospel is the *earliest* word-picture of Jesus that we have. It carries accounts of experienced events; added is much of the striking preaching-material of Peter, the greatest among the apostles. Indeed, young Mark stood so close to Peter's secret heart, that he called him, 'Mark, my son.' (1 Peter 5: 13) 'If,' as Dr. Barclay adds, 'Mark's Gospel was written shortly after Peter died, its date will be about A.D.65.' We may put it this way — 'Mark is the nearest approach we will ever possess to an eye-witness account of the life of Jesus.'

So this little book — for the reasons given — is a fitting start for a newcomer. More than this, it is a wonderful little book on which *to go on*. Sir John Lawrence — brought up in a liberal Christian family, reading Greats at Oxford — makes that clear. 'When the last glow of Faith had faded from the horizon,' said he, 'the world seemed by contrast inexpressably cold and dreary ... Then I considered the fact that if nothing was proved, equally nothing was disproved. Ought I not to look again at Christian belief?

'So I got out my Greek Testament, and began to read St. Mark's Gospel ... When I was about half-way through, I began to ask myself, "Who then was Jesus? Was he more than a man?" After that I was over the top of the hill.'

For Mark, of course, not only spoke for himself — a young man moving about — or for his friend, Peter. He did not live in a human void, or write in a void. By this time, he was able to convey the story of Jesus, as understood and cherished in Christian circles — the early belief concerning historical facts. And more than that, Mark balanced in his graphic telling of Jesus, *the human and the Divine.* His Gospel is much more than a mere hero-story; it begins with the striking words: 'The Gospel of Jesus, *the Son of God.*' And throughout, the awe and wonder which He evoked in Mark's mind and spirit, are recorded. 'They' — the worshippers in the synagogue — 'were astonished at His doctrine' (Ch. 1: 22). 'They were amazed' (Ch. 1: 27). And this was not limited to the crowds gathered; it was even more, the experience of His disciples about Him. And nowhere could there have been less likely witnesses. To start with, they were mostly Jews, instructed from childhood up, that God existed uniquely *alone.* This foundation point of all their teaching was literally woven into the very texture of their being. Yet here was their young Master claiming to be *one with God*! At first it must have sounded preposterous! But the evidence was so overwhelming, that they accepted it — in spite of the fact that they knew where He grew up, and knew the members of His family in their modest home in Nazareth. He admitted this, in a saying: 'No prophet is without honour, save in his own country.' He yet dared to say: 'The Son of Man hath power on earth to forgive sins' (Ch. 2: 10). And again: 'Whosoever shall lose his life for My sake and the Gospel's, shall save it' (Ch. 8. 35). And when later, the High Priest asked Him: 'Art Thou the Christ, the Son of the Blessed?' He said, 'I am; and ye shall see the Son of Man sitting at the right hand of power, and coming with the clouds of heaven.' (Ch. 14: 61–62). These claims were *either those of a self-deluded egoist, or they were true*; and that against the daily setting which they shared closely with Him, camping out-of-doors, travelling daily amongst people, becoming tired, sleeping in the end of the boat, thirsty, hungry, and finally praying in anguish in His familiar spot in the Garden, then flayed and tormented with a mock trial, stripped, and hanged between two thieves, on a Cross.

Despite their life-long training, and close association, they believed that He was no mere man among men — He was God among men, *very God, and very man*! This, Mark makes plain!

Once, Thomas Jefferson edited and published 'an abridged New Testament' for the Indians, 'unembarrassed by matters of fact and faith beyond their comprehension'. It consisted of the life-story and ethical teaching of Jesus, as a good man, *with all the divine factors left out*.

But Mark's little Gospel is not that kind of book — such a book cannot be called a Gospel at all. What Mark wrote for his fellow-Christians, and for us, was something very different. So it lives! Mark meant us to know that Jesus was not just a messenger of God, as many have been messengers before. At His baptism, the voice of God had been heard saying to Him: 'Thou art My beloved Son.' (Ch. 1: 11) and on the Mount of Transfiguration, the three disciples accompanying Him, heard God say: 'This is My beloved Son.' (Ch. 9: 7). One has no need to fear that in stressing Christ's divinity, one is somehow reducing His humanity. In the words of Viscount Hailsham, Q.C., of our day: 'Only a God who has suffered as a man can help us . . . Only a man who has truly born God's image on his personality can give us courage . . . He *must be a real man, and he must be a real God*. No imaginary Redeemer can work the miracle. Only a figure of history will serve. A real stone rolled away from a real tomb, in a real garden, at a real moment of time.'

10

From Crisis to Communion

I made one of the earliest air-trips from Adelaide to Alice Springs — a thousand miles into the heart of the Australian continent. When I first agreed to go, it seemed that I would have to travel by train, five-and-a-half days up across the Desert. It was much easier to reach the 'cinnabar centre' by air, though it was a bumpy trip. I think Padre Griffiths, with whom I travelled — who had given half a life-time to the Inland — and I were the only two who escaped the misery of air-sickness. We were too intent on all that we passed above, and all that we planned to do. Though the next five days offered 109° in the shade.

Planes pass to and fro regularly now — and usually in comfort, though a little while back, Reverend D. F. L. Harris — agent of the Bible Society — had an unenviable experience, coming back from Alice Springs. The Jet 727, in which he was travelling, had trouble at take-off, when a tyre burst. The pilot had quickly to jettison his fuel load, and make an emergency landing. In time, a relief plane took on the passengers. A nasty experience! Seated beside Mr. Harris was a Western Australian farmer, as it happened — the two men did not know each other; but as the United Bible Societies' *News and Views* reported, they fell to talk. The farmer's opening comment on their experience, was: '*I was so scared — I very nearly prayed.*'

Many do pray, of course, in *a crisis situation*. Clarence Day speaks of his own father — not a man of prayer. In a crisis moment, he says: 'Apparently now that he was in trouble, his thoughts turned to God. "Have mercy!" he was heard shouting indignantly: "I say have mercy, damn it!"' '

But this is not a modern attitude; the Psalmist knew it — he spoke of 'they that go down to the sea in ships, and do business

in great waters ... They mount up to heaven, they go down
again to the depths: their soul is melted because of trouble.
They reel to and fro, and stagger like a drunken man, and are
at their wits' end. Then they cry unto the Lord' (Psalm
107: 23–28). And those of us who have battled through a
prolonged storm at sea, night and day, know what he means:
and what George Herbert, nearer to our own day, means
when he says: 'He that will learn to pray, let him go to sea.'
Crisis-prayer comes easier to some, than to the scared Australian
farmer on the Jet 727. They are called, perhaps, to the bed-side
of a loved member of the family; they suffer an accident, or a
stroke; or a bomb blasts the long-loved security out of the
building which houses home. It is a crisis situation — a
moment when instinctively they reach out for support and help
like the Psalmist's men 'at their wits' end'. His fellow Hebrews
were essentially landsmen — some went 'down to the sea in
ships', but most were afraid of it. It spelled separation, unaccountable might, and devastation. When John, on the Isle of
Patmos, looked to a good time to come, in his vision, he said:
'There shall be no more sea!' That represented bliss to him.
For all we know, he might, as well as this general fear shared by
his fellowmen, have had a personal experience.

I remember hearing General William Dobbie, of Malta,
tell of the most critical time of World War II. He urgently
needed rolling-stock for the removal of troops to a threatened
position. He took up his phone; but when he explained his
crisis to the officer responsible, he was told that there was no
stock available. What did Dobbie do? In his crisis, he prayed.
To use his own words: 'I hung up the receiver and knelt down
in my office at Mongreuil, and laid the matter before God.
"It is absolutely necessary that we should carry out this move
— please help." ' 'Shortly afterwards,' he went on, 'the telephone rang and the officer in charge of rolling-stock was
speaking again. "The most extraordinary thing has happened.
Sufficient rolling-stock has suddenly and quite unexpectedly
become available, and we can carry out the move." ' But
General Dobbie, of course, was a man of prayer, and it was
natural practice for him to face a crisis with prayer; this is not
arguing that it will be always successful, or otherwise. Many
crisis prayers have been answered; there are countless instances,

reaching back to Peter, the fisherman, who prayed once dripping-wet in the sea. He was afraid, and beginning to sink, he cried, 'Lord, save me!' Our Lord, in giving his disciples what we call The Lord's Prayer, did not say: '*If* you pray . . .' He said, '*When* you pray' say this and this. He knew we would — if only in a crisis.

But prayer is very much more than this. Above all, it is *communion with God, the Father of our spirits*. A priest working in the slums of Calcutta tells of visiting a young girl whose faith was very real to her. She was in a Mission hospital. One afternoon, she lay so long with her eyes shut, that a nurse came to see what was going on. As she touched her patient, she opened her eyes. 'Have you been asleep?' she asked. 'No', came the answer, 'I was praying.' 'What were you asking for?' she added, to receive the answer: 'Oh, I wasn't *asking* for anything — I was just loving Him.'

Communion with the God Who created us, and who cares for us, is at every level of age and experience, as real. It is a family relationship — an earthly child who is communing with the Heavenly Father Who is holy love. Inmost thoughts, inward desires, human fears may all there be shared. If we get 'things' as well — this is an extra blessing. God interpenetrates the universe, as Creator and Father, and when the least of His family, by faith, seeks out His presence, His will, His power, in prayer, something happens.

A little while back, Dr. N. Jerome Stowell — a leading nuclear scientist — broadcast his conviction on this point. He said: 'With a delicate instrument which we have devised we can measure the wave-length of the brain. Recently we checked the emanations from the brain of a woman near death. She was praying at the time, and we could tell that something about her was reaching towards God. The meter registered 500 positive. This is fifty-five times the power registered by a fifty-kilowatt broadcast station sending a message around the world.' He adds, reflecting on this: 'We are on the threshold of spiritual discoveries. No one can fathom the literal pull a Christian exerts when he is in personal contact with God. It is tangible far beyond the comprehension of morality. It is similar, in one sense, to that which we know as radar. These experiences have caused me to turn to God. I have been a

Christian only a short time, and I know little of the way. This I do know — the things of God are positive ... The world little realises the impact of believing prayer. *It is a moving of the resources of the Infinite.*'

Prayer is not just something you say — it is an attitude during the whole of life; it is an experience of total reality, that bestows here and now on all our common affairs, a new dimension of power, of love, of beauty. I can't fashion for myself an adequate summing-up, so I will be content to make Paul's words my own: 'What am I to do? I will pray with the spirit and I will pray with the mind also; I will sing with the spirit and I will sing with the mind also' (I Corinthians 14: 15, R.S.V.). Sometimes, of course, prayer is just a responsive silence; to make this discovery, in this brash, noisy world is a 'shaft of sunlight'.

Sometimes, I find, I have to pray in a crisis; sometimes I have to pray in discomfort, with 'pins and needles' in my knees; but prayer is generally as real — and sometimes a lot more so — when I can pray relaxed in a chair, lying still out-of-doors, or walking, forgetful of my body.

II

'The Fifth Gospel'

I hardly dreamed that a day would come when I would walk in that little land that knew the earthly likeness of God's Son. It came as a gloriously rich widening of my reading of the Scriptures. Renan's observation suddenly came true: 'The Holy Land is the Fifth Gospel.' An unforgettable way of putting it!

Before leaving home to fly to Palestine — that little land, but a hundred-and-forty miles long, by eighty at its widest, my friend and I had already received a hint of the disquiet there.

The Mandelbaum Gate, we understood, was not a gate at all, but a barbed-wire division, with an armed guard on both sides of the frontier. We accordingly arranged to cross there — stepping over 'No man's land' with its aura of evil — from the Jordan side of Jerusalem, after our stay, to the Israel side of the city, and the country.

To manage this, we had been served by our Government with *two* passports each. This surprised us. And our Airways also supplied us each with *two* rolls of tickets. It seemed we might not offer for the scrutiny of the Jewish guard any document that Arab eyes had looked upon; and conversely, no Arab guard wanted to scrutinise any document that Jewish eyes had looked upon.

When we had gone to our doctor before leaving home, for travel injections, I had asked: 'Is there any difference in having it done in the thigh, instead of the arm? Last time I travelled, I had it in the thigh, and suffered swelling and pain and deep discoloration. If it is effective, I'd like to have it in the arm this time — left arm, as I shall be busy up till the last minute. 'He looked at my itinerary. 'You're going to Palestine? Well, we'll be doing it in the arm, anyway,' said he, adding, 'we used to do it in the thigh, till one of our lady-passengers found on reaching the Mandelbaum Gate, that the young guard wouldn't accept her injection-certificate as proof — he wanted to see "the place". So we always do it in the arm now.'

In crossing, we met with no difficulties. We stayed near the troublesome 'Gate', at St. George's Hostel, at the Cathedral, in its beautiful calm, sharing meals, talks, and trips about the city with other Christians. And when we were ready to cross over, we offered our second passports and rolls of tickets.

Since this was our first visit, we were fortunate to be quietly guided to many special sites, by a retiring missionary staying, as we were, at St. George's — making what would be, she said, her 'last trip'. When we moved out beyond the Holy City, she shared with us a car St. George's hired for us, and a picnic lunch that we could eat like first-century pilgrims, under the blue-grey shadows of the olive-trees.

*　　*　　*

Beginning — as seemed fitting — at the beginning, we paid a visit to Bethlehem. When the time comes that life's shadows are long drawn out, and only a few experiences are remembered, I shall remember that day, as the handful of shepherds 'keeping watch over their flocks by night', must have remembered their unique experience there. We were able to look down over the Shepherds' Fields, as we made our way first to the Church of the Nativity. It was preparation of mood to find ourselves in Manger Square, in the centre of the town with its white houses, before the Church. (An early tradition had described the birth-place as a cave, at the rear of the Inn; and Origen, in A.D.215 had underlined its acceptance, with the words: 'They still show the cave in Bethlehem where He was born.')

Never will we forget the door through which we entered the Church standing over the birthplace. In world-travels we had entered many doors — into homes, apartments, palaces, plain cottages — but none was like this. Once, it had been a large door, arched high; but casual passers-by, straying beasts, and infidels riding proudly, had entered there. So those who cared greatly, had taken great blocks of honey-coloured matching stone, and reduced its size. Till the only way we could enter — one by one, was each with bowed head — and nothing could be more fitting. (I have a photograph of Rene making her humble entry.)

On the floor of the Cave within, craftsmen's skill had fastened a Star, and round it an inscription which, in transla-tion, reads: '*Here Jesus Christ was born of the Virgin Mary.*'

That birth — in that humble place — has become 'the hinge of history'; in choice New Testament words (Galatians 4: 4, one of my favourite passages) '*When the fullness of Time was come, God sent forth His Son, made of a woman . . . to redeem.*' 'Some religions,' as Dr. C. H. Dodd had reminded me, 'can be indifferent to historical fact, and move entirely upon the plane of timeless truth. Christianity cannot. It rests upon the affirmation that a series of events happened, in which God revealed Himself in action, for the salvation of men.'

In little Bethlehem — as I have told at some length in my autobiography, *The Sun is High* — we moved from the Birth Cave, to find in a home, proof of the new worth of little child-ren, which came into the world that first Christmas. They were little blind children, with whom we shared cold drinks, joyous laughter, and stories. And before we parted, they sang for us one song they knew, that we knew: 'O little town of Bethlehem!' It was an unforgettable moment, for we were in the midst of it — of its compassion, as well as its geography. One had set it down in simple words:

Still Bethlehem the town
Lies where it lay long years ago . . .
Still, brown-faced children play
Through crooked streets
And wander on the hills,
Still men sow seed, and harvest grain,
Still women bake,
Still runs life's endless circle
Round and round,
And common days are filled with common toil.

But all the world
Goes the more bravely to its task
Because once, long ago,
A little Child was born
In Bethlehem.

[Anon]

*   *   *

Now, all births are viewed by us in the light of that Bethlehem birth. In *Naught For Your Comfort*, Trevor Huddlestone describes a cold December night in Sophiatown, on the fringe of Johannesburg. Families huddled in flimsy shacks. That night a husband returned from work to find his shanty dismantled by the authorities, and his wife in labour in front of a brazier. Their baby was born under a canopy of stars. Says Huddlestone: 'In that dejected scene in Edith Street, the picture of Bethlehem came to life.' For there was nothing 'pretty-pretty' about that first Christmas in Bethlehem. 'There was no room for them in the Inn.' Its background was as dark — the census decree from Caesar Augustus, Emperor of Rome, heartless, and removed from personal care for the common people, his dominion extending out beyond the local scene, and

lands of the Mediterranean, over seas eastward to Asia. All
this, made up — as Luke took some pains to make clear — evil,
and fear in high places, instability in local administration,
apathy in domestic matters. But then, he added one fact
more — and in our disquiet world, it is good to remember it.
'There were,' he says, '*in the same country*, shepherds abiding
in the fields, keeping watch over their flock by night' (Luke
2: 8). 'In the same country' — doesn't that strike you? Evil,
undoubtedly, was as dark as could be — but 'in the same
country there were shepherds'. They represent the ordinary,
honest-to-goodness people in every situation, evil, powerful,
blatant! And because there are 'shepherds' still — alert, and
likely to be overlooked — the statement of a fellow New
Zealander, Dr. Alan Brash, serving through the World Church,
reached me full of significance. 'It is wrong today', said he,
'to think of Moscow as unconditionally Red evil. It is not! The
Orthodox Church is now much stronger than in 1917 —
twenty thousand Christian communities meet for worship in
Russia.'

God had His 'shepherds' still!

* * *

From Bethlehem, our way led presently to Nazareth where the
Lad grew up. The little town with its white houses, still stands
enthroned on the hills, as in His day, the spear-like cypresses
alert, supported by fig and olive-trees.

As we walked towards the Christian hospital serving in His
Name, and other points of interest beyond the handful of
modest streets, we came upon a carpenter at his task — his
tools, and scope of service little changed since Joseph's day.
And then we paused to allow me to capture a photograph
of a youngish mother and her small son at Mary's Well. This
had ever been the only water-supply in Nazareth — to it,
Mary herself, and her Lad must often have come, to draw
water, as part of simple home-making.

And it seemed as fitting to walk up the white dusty path to
the Church of Jesus-Adolescent — chapel of a school for boys,
with a figure of the Adolescent Jesus set high above the altar.
To its site on the hilltop, under wide skies, He must often
have climbed before any building was raised.

Later, we were shown the spot where His angered townsfolk tried to cast Him over, after His first sermon in His home-town — presenting the revolutionary message of His Kingdom to be: 'The Spirit of the Lord is upon Me, because He hath appointed Me to preach deliverence to the captives, and recovering of sight to the blind, to set at liberty them that are bruised, to preach the acceptable year of the Lord!' At first, they were charmed: 'All spoke well of Him, and wondered at the gracious words which proceeded out of His mouth.' (Luke 4: 22, R.S.V.) Then they had second thoughts; it was more than they could take. In that moment, it suddenly dawned upon them, that His words were both penetrating and far-reaching, involving their own way of life. In fury, they tried to get rid of Him! Mercifully, He escaped, before they could cast Him to death over the nearby steep place.

*   *   *

One of our high moments, was at 'the lowest hospital in the world' — the missionary hospital beside the shimmering waters of Galilee, the Lake, six-hundred-and-eighty feet below sea-level.

We journeyed to it, with Dr. Bernard Walker — retiring after nineteen years service — in his car making a friendly round of calls; and he prepared our eyes and hearts for that memorable experience.

I was able to move through the hospital's kindly wards — with a smile here and there, because I could do no more, want of skill and language preventing. One night, when it was cool. I was asked to speak to a group of nurses off duty. When I had finished, there were questions, and we sat late into the velvety darkness, with coffee. They had tales to tell, too; and I encouraged them.

When their first X-ray unit was installed, I learned, there had come a rich Damascene for medical help — pleading poverty. Doctor and staff were all doubtful about the truth of his claims. In the dark-room later — aided by their new 'magic' — a little mirthfully, they were able to count the gold coins in his voluminous pockets!

But there were other tales. One of the very young nurses wrote into her report, I learned, a word which showed up her

stumbling spelling. But what she wrote was actually memorable: for Doctor's Consultation Room, she wrote, all unwittingly, a good Bible word. She called it his '*Consolation
Room*', meaning something beyond medical aid — 'spiritual
refreshing and strengthening of the heart'.

Whatever might be argued about some of the Holy places,
there could be no question about the waters and gentle hills of
Galilee. One day — as He had done many times — we crossed
the lake, and ate fish on the other side. One night we saw the
full moon rise over its waters. To waken early, as we were
able, and later to walk those grassy slopes in quest of refreshment, was to recall His love of wild things, and His teaching of
God's care — through birds and flowers.

It was easy, after that visit, to write —

Under the wide sky day after day
is language old before man's birth —
breathing in tall grasses,
as the winds pass through —
owning no place in any dictionary on earth.

I sing glory, to God for grasses,
gifts of Time, spelling out His ways —
as ever in Galilee,
breezes loosed as now,
lilies and birds part of Christ's paean of praise!

[R.F.S.]

12

Close to Life

Whilst in Jerusalem, the old City upon which so much turns,
we made a point of seeking out the Church of the Paternoster,
high up, overlooking the City. More than any other, it is closely

linked with the Prayer that in our world today is more often upon human lips than any other. Our Lord gave it to His questioning disciples hereabouts — now known to us as 'The Lord's Prayer'.

The Byzantines built a church on the spot — later replaced. And coloured tiles may still be seen set into the wall of the quiet cloisters — its petitions expressed there in thirty-five different languages. Never now, an hour passes, by day or night, but somewhere, in some language, that Prayer rises to God. It is taught to the very young; it serves as a challenge to the middle-aged; it ministers comfort to the old when the shadows fall. Twenty centuries have not exhausted it; it has still a place within the usage of each section of the World Church, in every Christian service from baptism to burial.

'Last night, going to bed alone,' said Edwin Muir, poet of our day, 'I suddenly found myself (I was taking off my waist-coat) reciting the Lord's Prayer in a loud, emphatic voice — a thing I had not done for many years — with deep urgency and profound, disturbed emotion. When I went on, I grew more composed . . . every word had a strange fitness of meaning which astonished and delighted me. It was late: I had sat up reading; I was sleepy; but as I stood in the middle of the floor half-undressed, saying the Prayer over and over, meaning after meaning sprang from it, overcoming me again with joyous surprise!'

To its all-embracing petitions, we add our own from time to time, as occasion arises. Dr. Frank Laubach — our modern champion of literacy — confessed, when I listened to him in London, that he constantly added: 'Lord, forgive us for looking at the world with dry eyes — and empty hands.' It would be well-nigh impossible to think of a more timely addition. Today, there is so much cruelty, and so much casualness — our newspaper headlines, radio and T.V. news-reports underline this painfully. Happily, Christian compassion has by no means died out — indeed, a recent report tells us that there are over seventy-thousand registered charities in Britain alone! Most of these go back to The Parable of the Good Samaritan!

Rene and I journeyed down the road he knew — from Jerusalem to Jericho, two thousand two hundred feet above sea-level, to a thousand and three hundred feet below! It is still a winding road. But when our Lord began His famous parable with the words: 'A certain man went down from Jerusalem to Jericho', it must have struck dread into the hearts of those who listened. News reached them day after day concerning one and another 'fallen among thieves'. Stripped and wounded and left half-dead, many a poor wretch lay there. His parable was of such an one — passed by a Priest, and presently by a Levite. Then a man He called attention to — a Samaritan — chanced that way. Without stopping to argue the prior importance of his own affairs, or how bothersome — not to say, dangerous — delay could be, he set about rendering aid. Likely enough, the robbers were not far away — even at that moment, in hiding waiting for a second victim. The 'Jews', he well knew, 'had no dealings with the Samaritans', but he did not let this racial-discrimination hinder him. To him, the situation was a human situation, calling for compassion. (To-day, it would be as if a German risked his life to help a Jew.)

Of the other two, some modern cynic has suggested, that they were likely hurrying to journey's end to 'attend a committee-meeting of the Distressed Travellers' Aid Society'. One thing stands certain — they did nothing. It was the 'outsider', the Samaritan who shone as the hero of the piece.

Today, the road down to Jericho, with all its hazards, runs through our cities, and suburban streets, through our factories, offices, club-rooms, kitchens. It is where loneliness, ignorance, superiority slays. A cynic of our day has spoken all too truly in saying: 'We would each like to be The Good Samaritan — *if it wasn't for the time, the trouble, and the two-pence!*'

*   *   *

His Parable has survived — though there was not much compassion anywhere shown for the Divine Story-teller Himself. Reflecting on this, I came across a passion-flower — and photographed it in colour — on the outside wall of the Garden of Gethsemane! I was coming down the ankle-breaking pathway that led from the Mount of Olives. (As a child, one Easter, my mother had tried to explain to me the symbolism of the Passion-flower — at its heart, a representation of the Cross; another part she likened to His crown of thorns;

with another part looking like a scourge; five stamens were there to represent His wounds; and the flower's dark red in another part suggested spilled blood.)

Lifting the heavy latch on the Garden gate, Rene and I went into Gethsemane — with its eight ancient olive-trees, gnarled and bluey-green, still alive there. An old Franciscan brother with great gentleness, moved among them, tidying up the grass verges. These venerable trees, are very likely heirs of those that sheltered our Lord on that fateful night. The olive, by nature, experts assure us, sends up shoots about the parent tree always before it dies, to hand on its life. Certainly there is a promise in the Book of Psalms, to a man who 'fears the Lord' — his children, the promise says, shall be 'as olive plants about his table'.

*   *   *

Later, we walked in the streets — and as unexpectedly, came upon another reminder of our Lord's Passion. I knocked at a door in a wall, and it was opened to us by a gentle Sister of Sion. She led us along a cool passage, down some steps, through a church, down further steps, and on. Then she stopped. It was dark about us — since we were by this time, so far below ground-level. Walking ahead, at one point and another, she switched on a light.

Now we were standing, with hearts hushed, upon the flagstones of the courtyard of The Palace of Antonia, where during His trial, our Lord had stood before Pilate. No one could argue against this site — any more than against the hills of Galilee. Distances were short between here and the Garden of Gethsemane, where the soldiers arrested Him. They brought Him in — and their duty done, moved off from the house of the High Priest, to their barracks here within the Castle of Antonia.

Awed we stood, and the Gospel records of that night's dastardly deeds came to life — a light flickering, it seemed, on the face of each man involved. Terrible things were suddenly revealed — pride, greed, hunger for power, fear, sadism. False witnesses had joined Annas, Caiaphas, Pilate, not to mention Judas and Peter, in that night's work. Bored with waiting, as the hours passed, the soldiers had filled in time in

their customary way. There were no words to tell by my lips
the shock of the moment when the gentle Sister of Sion stooped
and lifted up a piece of matting at our feet, revealing in the
scarred pavement, the marks of the soldiers' game, *Basilikos*,
Game of the King! 'Here they are,' said she, pointing to the
deeply cut marks just where we stood, on the great flagstones!

Again — out at last on the narrow street — we followed
'The Via Dolorosa', as the soldiers had done, between that
hour of boredom, and the hour of crucifixion, when they had
'cast lots for His clothes'. They were justly entitled by law
to their Prisoner's private property; but this cloak was too
fine to rend for shares, so they cast lots for it. It was like His
life, woven without seam from end to end!

On Friday, at three o'clock — as the custom is — we joined
a little company of Franciscans who trod, for Christ's sake,
the modern Via Dolorosa — pausing for silent prayer a moment
or two at each station of the Cross. There was no pretending
— at this date, we are on the Easter-side of the Cross. The
terrible experience of suffering which He knew, somewhere
out amid the rabble, would give way in time to Life! A triumphant verse from the Book of Acts (1: 3) leapt to the forefront of my mind: 'He showed Himself *alive after His passion*
by many infallible proofs!'

He knew at no time now, any reason to say the word 'Goodbye',
that He had used to a chosen company of friends earlier. Mark
reported: 'After saying *Goodbye* to them, He went up the hill to
pray' (Mark 6: 46, Moffatt). Goodbye is a very human word —
as we all know to our grief, as a train pulls out, or a plane sets
off for a country we will never visit, or we return home after
the death of someone beloved.

When Death had done its worst with Christ, He rose in
triumph — talked again with His friends over many days —
and ascended. From that leave-taking, we read that those who
loved Him returned without grief; indeed, we read, 'they
worshipped Him, and returned to Jerusalem *with great joy*!'
(Luke 24: 52). This revelation comes as 'a shaft of sunlight'
across earth's darkest hours. *It carries an assurance of triumph,
as no other!*

When I later pondered on these things — and gathered up all
as triumphant realities — I called my poem: '*Peter remembers*':

He came striding along the water's edge,
     clothed in man's five senses —
     The boats beached, I was mending snagged nets,
     scaley, and deep-sea washed.
     And soon — I was snatching up cloak and sandals
     ready to walk the world with Him.

I never met another like Him —
     as straight in thought as in manly stance,
     wind in His hair, kissing His cheek,
     His eyes going straight to the point.
     Again and again, *my* words tumbled each other,
     but there was no hiding secrets from Him.

Days passed in dusty towns, the sick clamouring —
     nights under the stars, as we camped,
     so robust He was, so sure, He kept turning
     life's water into wine.
     Mothers and children sought Him, at ease,
     along with lepers, and the learned.

My fisherman's eyes were half-shut, limited —
     and there came a week I could never have guessed.
     Each of His words sadly distorted — spelling out
     the dark Gardèn, circled thorn and death.
     One of our company grasped in palm, and heart,
     coins as terrible as thirty suns blazing.

And we all scattered, to follow afar off —
     caught in madness, committed to grief.
     Seeking comfort at a fire of coals,
     a servant-girl threw a noose of words about my
     neck.
     Pilate — so final his judgment — faltered,
     washed his hands — a dust-bowl in his heart.

And suddenly there was a Cross to be carried
     up a cruel Hill, crowds jeering —
     He was king still, though covered now in sweat.
     The tumult echoing up the walled street

waned only when He hung there stark against the
  sky —
a thin uncertain company standing by.

'The cruel day's end brought His body down — broken,
  limp;
   each who dared His friendship
   fashioning his own silent epitaph;
   staggering bewilderment and grief
   slammed doors for safety; the dank grave
   holding His body.

Spices weigh heavy when the heart is numb —
   but the women, purposeful, slipped out early
   ere the sun's arrows were laid across the grass;
   so were first to hear a step — and a name spoken;
   before John and I could come running
   to find the stone rolled away.

Let soldiers argue, and those they serve —
   there was no shadow on that dawn.
   I heard that Voice again — that very Voice,
   bereft of love no longer — broken out of Death!
   And I knew what I must do, and where
   through all the world, my stumbling feet must take
     me!

[R.F.S.]

13

Light on a Vocation

I have circled the earth several times since I started to carry a passport. As occupation, it gives my dual vocation, 'Deaconess-Author' — unique, perhaps, set down as distinctively as that.

A young receptionist thought so, at least, one day in Athens, as I first stepped into Greece, and sought lodgings.

Poised at her desk, behind a large, leather-bound record, she took my passport into her hands, and began to scrutinise it closely. '*Deaconess-Author*', she repeated aloud, after having read it silently: 'Deacon — preacher? Deaconess — woman preacher? Author — writer of books. Deaconess-Author, woman-preacher, writer of books? *How v-e-r-y p-e-c-u-l-i-a-r*!'

Peculiar or not, those dual strands have long made up my vocation.

In many places today, the word 'vocation' has come to be associated entirely with some kind of ministry within the Church — with the exception of a life-work of teaching, or service to one's fellow-humans, through medicine; the corollary being that the great majority who feel no such exalted call, have in reality no 'vocation'. Early, I am thankful to say, *it dawned upon me how far this was removed from essential Christian values*. The doctrine of vocation, I saw, was concerned with the largest single block of one's waking hours — the time spent in occupational work.

Christ Himself was a workman — toiling at a bench, wood-shavings and sawdust falling about Him — meeting the material needs of His fellows. He made woodenchests for the village-girls, one by one, as His customers, as the time came for each, as a young bride, to set up home; He fashioned wooden plough-yokes for those whose work was with the soil, following oxen up and down under the high sun.

When the Young Carpenter was ready to set out on His preaching-ministry, it was, strikingly enough, to little Nazareth that He came — to launch His new work among those who had known Him longest, and best. He ran no risk in that, He knew — there was no likelihood that among the company that listened to His words, one would raise her voice to say: 'You remember the chest you made for me when I married, when I needed somewhere to store my linen — well, it's lid never fitted, it let in the moths!' *No!* Even had she found courage to say it, no housewife offered such a complaint. And no manly voice of deeper tones, was heard saying: 'Mr. Carpenter, I always had trouble with that ill-fitting yoke made for my beast. It galled its neck dreadfully — it never really fitted. *No!* The work which came from His bench was good work. This is confirmed in His choice of Nazareth as the starting-place for His public-ministry.

More than that: when He stepped down to the water-side, for John's baptism, a Voice from heaven was heard, saying in that moment a wonderful thing: 'This is My beloved Son, in Whom I am well-pleased!'

What had He done that so pleased God? He hadn't preached a single sermon then, raised a single person from the dead, reached out a healing hand to a single sufferer. What He had done was a day-to-day 'secular' task — if one likes to call it that — dealing with human needs, taking orders, handling money, helping support His family-home. (It was, to me, a clear 'shaft of sunlight' when I saw this for the first time.)

From the beginning of discipleship, men and women who followed Him, had each to ask: 'Does it matter what I choose to do? Can I do this or this?' Clearly, one could not be a heathen priest, a maker of incense for customary sacrifices, a gladiator; even a builder could be caught in a contract for a temple, a tailor for making robes for a heathen priest. A Christian was bound to give thought to these matters — to cut himself off from much of the social and religious life of his time; and any man who, for even the best of reasons, stands aloof, cannot hope to be popular. But none who followed would commit himself to any work which robbed his fellow-man of his dignity, rightful gain, or in any way hazarded his home and family-life. He must choose another.

And that still holds in the very different setting of today — one must choose a job that is creative, not destructive, 'a job' — as Katherine Mansfield put it — 'that he can show to God.' A young sixth-former, keen on science, may well wonder about a future in the modern paraphernalia of destruction — in flame-throwers, in nuclear-weapons, in the elements of bacteriological warfare. But all careers offer some kind of challenge. Whatever the choice, one thing is certain, God is as interested in typewriters and shovels, as in litanies and sermons, in screw-drivers and nursing text-books, as in Communion-vessels.

College-trained and set apart in a holy service for one strand of my vocation, I have never considered it holier than the other that I have forwarded by the pounding of a type-writer, preparing manuscripts for editors, checking tedious galley-proofs, and attending to the business required between an author and publisher. Tens of thousands in offices use the same tools daily; but that makes no difference. Derrick Greeves tied these two strands together for me when he spoke of 'a certain distinguished worker in the Church who began his missionary service as a young teacher in West Africa. When he left his home Church, he was asked by the leaders of that Church if he would like to have a Service of Dedication before he left. He replied that he would, but only on one condition, that his friend, Leonard, was also given the same honour and glory and blessing. Now Leonard was going into a local engineering factory on the Great West Road. 'This,' confesses Derrick Greeves, 'was too much of a stretch of vision for the leaders concerned — and the matter was left in abeyance.'

A thousand pities! Our world needs good Christian engineering, responsible men at the Corporation Water-works, that the water supplied might be fit to drink: responsible house-builders and cabinet-makers, as in the profession of the young Carpenter of Nazareth. Why drive a wedge between forms of service, done 'to the glory of God'? The Report from the Lambeth Conference a year or two back, had something to say about this: 'It will usually be more valuable service,' ran the statement, 'to take an active part in a trade-union, on the shop-floor, or in administration, than to count the collection.' A statement as striking — and even more positive — was issued by the Second Assembly of the World Churches. 'The real battles of the Faith today,' it said 'are being fought in factories, shops, offices and farms, in political parties and government agencies, in countless homes, in the press, radio and television, and in the relationship of nations.'

I know, of course, that for many, work is just 'a necessary evil', a curse — God doesn't come into it, nor does any free, glad human choice. One can only be moved with pity for such. I know how many around me feel that way — they have admitted as much.

The tools of modern work have become increasingly more sophisticated; but the true spirit of 'vocation' need in no way be affected by this. It is the motivation with which one approaches the work that makes all the difference. The brief, meaningful petition by Thomas à Kempis rises immediately to my lips, whether I set about either form of service that has long combined in my 'vocation'. Morning by morning, I bow my head a moment, before 'yaffling away' at my type-writer, to pray: 'O Lord, in the simplicity of my heart, I offer myself to Thee today, to be Thy servant for ever, and to be a sacrifice of perpetual praise. AMEN.'

14

The Reality of the Resurrection

We were joined in Athens by a friend whose college was in war-torn Beirut. She was delayed, and we lingered late into the night, waiting for her at the airways bus-stop in the empty street. It was a relief when clutching hand-luggage, she stumbled out at our feet, and with a score of questions on our lips, we were able to escort her to her room in the hotel where we were to stay the night. By this time, much of it had gone — and it was quite two o'clock before we could think of sleep — but we parted with the understanding that we would meet in an hour or so, to share one of the world's great sights, sun-rise over the Acropolis!

A few minutes short of four o'clock — warmly clad — we three, half-awake, groped down the dimly-lighted stairs, each carrying her shoes. The moment we reached the foyer, the night-porter suddenly roused, shouted after us. We might well have appeared to him to be departing without settling our dues. In loud whispers — and it's strange how one always speaks loudly where there is a matter of language, as though one might be better understood that way. The porter's knowledge of English was wanting at many points; but as the words 'Acropolis', and 'sun-rise' were repeated, his eyes suddenly lightened. And allowing us to put on our shoes, he opened the big front door and led us into the street.

Soon — following his directions — we saw above Athens' noblest streets, and little taverns and houses, the ancient pillars of the Parthenon! With glory of another kind, we were able to match this sight, with the discovery of a street nearby, bearing the name of *Dionysius*! In that moment, Paul's record of his visit to the city, came alive. Since the beginning of time, the townspeople had never been wanting in curiosity.

Soon, Paul had them by the ears — tactfully paying tribute to their famous dialectical habits. 'Men of Athens, I perceive that in every way you are very religious.' (A fine compliment.) 'For as I passed along, and observed the objects of your worship, I found also an altar with this inscription: "To an unknown god". What therefore you worship as unknown, this I proclaim to you. The God who made the world and everything in it being Lord of heaven and earth...' (Acts 17: 22-24, R.S.V.) Paul's whole being was stirred in him, when he saw the city given over to idolatory. He knew what some of the Epicureans and Stoics before him were murmuring: ' "What will this babbler say?" Others said, "He seemeth to be a setter-forth of strange gods," because he preached unto them *Jesus and the Resurrection*.' ('Babbler', I recalled, literally meant 'seed-picker', Athenian slang for a philosophic picker-up of trifles, like a bird hopping over newly-turned soil.) But Paul was no 'babbler' — and even in our English version, his speech reads magnificently. (As soon as we got back, I made haste to turn it up in my New Testament. How vivid it was! How its challenge leaped out to meet me anew, as I stood on the very spot on Mars' hill — where today, is a bronze carrying the whole of that magnificent utterance in beautiful Greek lettering. 'When they heard of the Resurrection, some mocked ... others said, "We will hear thee again on this matter" ... howbeit certain clave unto him and believed, *among the which was Dionysius*.' Bless him! It was exciting to find nearby, that street named for one *who wasn't upset by mention of the Resurrection*!)

Today, as then, it stands at the very heart of Christianity! When Professor A. M. Hunter wrote *The Work and Word of Jesus*, he sent a copy of his book at her request to Her Majesty the Queen — now the Queen Mother. (The last chapter is centred on the Resurrection.) After a little interval, a letter carrying a confession came from Her Majesty. She wrote of the book she had enjoyed: 'I am sorry to say I read the last chapter first, which is, I know, dreadful cheating: but it makes a wonderful and hopeful background to the rest of the book, and I do not regret it. *Perhaps the light of the Resurrection will yet flood the world.*'

There might be reasons for varying opinions on *how* it happened — there was no human witness present to see the stone rolled away, and the triumphant Figure of the Young Man come forth. But there cannot be any doubt that He *did* come forth, the Resurrection *did* happen! The four Gospels report it at considerable length — small discrepancies only serving to strengthen its veracity, as in any series of reports of a public happening today — a faked story being always put together with more deliberate care, each turn of the story checked to carefully coincide.

And there are other proofs. When Paul wrote to his friends in Corinth — and spoke about the Resurrection — he was able to name some who lived through that great happening, and were still alive: 'He was seen of Cephas, then of the twelve; after that, He was seen of about five hundred brethren at once — of whom the greater part remain unto this present, but some are fallen asleep. After that, He was seen of James then of all the apostles. And last of all, He was seen of me also, as one born out of due season' (1 Corinthians 15: 5-8).

One of the most telling proofs lies in the living change in the disciples themselves — men reduced to bewildering despair and purposelessness — after this, possessed of an unalterable certainty, and garrisoned with a matchless courage before those very authorities who had been guilty of the Crucifixion. On the Resurrection, the Christian Church was founded — soon to honour the *first* day of the week as 'The Lord's Day' — celebrating the completion of man's Redemption, rather than on the *seventh*, the completion of Creation.

For myself, I am one with Bishops John Robinson and Hugh Montefiore, in their statement during a public discussion in Great St. Mary's in Oxford: 'The empty tomb appears in all four Gospels. We've got to consider how the story arose . . . If it didn't arise because it actually happened, how anybody could have made it up in the form in which it now appears is the difficulty . . . *I think the living Christ is the foundation of the Christian faith . . .'*

From time to time, men have made efforts to explain it away — but they involve each of them in an impossible credibility gap — and none could have re-made fear-stricken disciples, or brought up to this present time the Christianity we know. I can remember the moment when this reality burst upon me with the all-clarifying light of a revelation. And now I find it summed-up in the stirring statement of historian Arnold Toynbee: 'At the final ordeal of Death, few even of the would-be saviour gods have dared to put their title to the test, by plunging into the icy river. And now as we stand and gaze with our eyes fixed upon the farther shore, *a single Figure rises from the flood and straightway fills the whole horizon. There is the Saviour!'*

15

The Riches of Involvement

Amongst the Saints, who have followed Him most closely through the centuries, St. Francis has always stood first in my affection — and not only, I think, because the second name given me in baptism. chanced to be 'Frances', the feminine form of his own. Curiously, through the years, official documents have more often than not, come bearing *his* spelling. One morning a little while ago, I went to re-register my car — filling in the form, carefully in block-letters. At once, the official to whom I presented it, set about matching it with a card in his file. 'I must ask you to do this again', said he, 'you haven't given us your second name correctly.' 'But I have,' was

my answer, 'allow me to suggest that it is your record which is
at fault.' With that, he disappeared behind the scenes to check
with some other, and in a minute returned. 'The two forms
have to match,' said he, 'you must alter this.' It was now my
turn to be insistent. 'But this is correct — this name I have
lived with for sixty-odd years; I think you can trust me to
know its spelling.' With that, he disappeared again. When he
reappeared, it was to add: 'Our senior says that you can change
the card we have in the files, for a shilling.' 'But this mistake
is on your side,' said I. 'It is surely your responsibility to pay
the shilling.' Once more he disappeared — and reappeared.
And we parted with a smile and a nod.

When Ernest Raymond's *In the Steps of St. Francis* appeared
in my favourite book-shop, I carried home a copy. Never did
I dream that one day I would listen to it being read in the very
countryside St. Francis himself knew and loved, Assisi.
Rene and a friend and I spent five lovely days in the little
hill town of tiled roofs, with its harvest-fields below, where the
famous white oxen drew in laden drays. Nearby, the golden
stacks rose. We spent hours in the bluey-grey shade of the old
olive-trees, sharing our simple picnic-meals; and there we read
aloud Ernest Raymond's book, and rested. Throughout the little
town, with its irregular streets, high window-boxes of red
geraniums cast crisp shadow patterns on the sunny stone walls.

Again and again, we made our way downhill to the wide
gentleness of Spoleto's vale, where once the young Francis —
at wind's speed — had run to join his companions. Everyone
then knew the son of the cloth-merchant, as later everyone
knew 'the troubadour of Christ'.

A number of churches had been raised thereabouts, we
found — each marking out some never-to-be-forgotten experience in his life. One, I confessed, seemed a good deal too
grandiose for the simple-hearted Saint in his plain brown
habit, and girdle of rope — it was the many-arched San Fran-
cesco strikingly high on the eastern edge of the little town. At
the other extreme — and my favourite — was the tiny chapel
which had once stood in the woods, seven-and-a-half centuries
earlier. It had been old then — when Francis and his friends
accepted it as a gift from the Benedictines. It stood, keeping
company with their modest wattle and daub cells; and they

set about restoring its fabric with their own hands. Today, it is preserved from direct contact with the elements, beneath the immense arches of *Santa Maria degli Angeli* — the 'Church of St. Mary of the Angels'.

Offering pew-space for twenty to thirty worshippers, I seemed closest to the spirit of St. Francis in that tiny chapel, and paused there again and again, in silent meditation.

It had been to this spot that Clare — the beautiful eighteen-year-old who had fled her father's castle and grand life — came, after her conversion to simpler values. Midnight passed, it was on Monday following Palm Sunday, 1212, that the friars took their torches to light her through the woods, into the immediate care of the Benedictine nuns. In time, her own convent of the Poor Clares was founded.

In time, St. Francis's friends and followers grew in numbers, till they reached all over Italy. Their piety and deeds of mercy spoke for themselves. It has proved a timeless venture, and it was a moving experience to be in Assisi where it all began. We grew familiar with the brown habit and rope girdle, unchanged, being worn by members of the two Orders, about their affairs. The little chapel seemed to be a much more fitting place for the last resting-place of St. Francis, than the great basilica chosen. The only fact that comforted me was the knowledge that there were buried also four of his original disciples — Brother Leo, nicknamed 'the little lamp of God'; Brother Angelo, 'the gentle knight'; Brother Masseo, and Brother Rufino, so holy that Francis nick-named him 'Saint Rufino'.

Happily, in the upper church, the gifted Giotto in time, set out as he alone could, in twenty-eight frescoes, the story of the gay-hearted young spirit become Saint. Animals, birds, and humble hearts followed him closely, as did their shadows other men.

*   *   *

Treasuring this moving experience, I wrote: 'Harvest Days in Assisi' —

Problems bruise my mind, but not here —
in Saint Francis's setting, all is as golden
as a slat of sunlight through the door,
as simple as the creatures of God's giving.

Up on the hill, church-doors stand open,
the people going with a canticle of praise,
some from village homes in little streets,
some from the far world with eyes of curiosity.

Down here, near the kindly olives
is the water-trough, and at harvest
those faithful to God's earthy purpose
raise the golden stacks and guide the white oxen.

Long, abrasive centuries make no difference,
God's sun rises, and His seasons turn,
cupped in the friendly contour of the hills,
these simple things of the heart live on.

[R.F.S.]

*   *   *

The schoolboy who spoke of St. Francis of Assisi, as 'St. Francis the Sissy', plainly had no knowledge of his personality — his manly vigour as the cloth-merchant's son, his gaiety of spirit as Christ's troubadour. A pity! It may have been that he was 'a Saint', credited with loving care of outcasts and wild creatures, that put him off. I wish I'd asked.

It is true that Francis was credited with actually preaching to the creatures. 'My little brothers,' said he, to the birds about him, 'ye ought greatly to praise and love the Lord who created you, for He provides all that is necessary, giving you feathers for raiment and wings to fly with.' The birds, others said, listened reverently till he made the sign of the Cross, and gave them leave to be off. However they might claim that this affectionate, half-humorous relationship stands unique among mystics, it seems that Francis's love of the Creatures exceeded those of others. One thing that many did, which was wholly outside his relationship, was to detect a devil approaching in the shape of an animal, or bird.

The lovely story of Francis's death is re-told by Ernest Raymond, that we read under the olives:

His faithful disciples were with him at the end. They watched by him all that night; and the first light of Friday the second of October began to come ... But Francis could distinguish light from darkness no more, and thinking it was still Thursday he said, 'I should like you to bring me a loaf which we will break and eat together as our Master did the last Thursday before He died.'

'But this is not Thursday,' they told Him gently, 'it is Friday now.'

'I thought it was still Thursday.'

Still, the loaf was brought, and he broke it for them, and each ate his fragment, a symbol of his share in their common love.

'Now read to me the Gospel for Maundy Thursday,' said Francis. They fetched the Book and read that Gospel for the Thursday before Easter.

'All that day they saw him slowly sinking, but just as the sun of Saturday, October 3rd, 1226, was dropping down towards the mountains ... and as all noticed with joy, the larks were singing loudly in the last of the day, Francis was heard to sing, too ... Soon the watching brothers saw that he was dead. And, they wrote afterwards of the peace and happiness on his face. They wrote also '*that in the silence they heard the larks singing*'.

*   *   *

Countless figures have been erected, showing St. Francis with the creatures — but much more to the point, is his gentle spirit spread the whole world round.

I was once making my way homewards by public transport, after a busy, tiring day in my own city, when a fine-looking young man seated himself beside me. He was obviously excited about something, and ready to talk. 'I hope you won't think me slightly mad,' said he, 'but I've just saved the life of a bumble-bee — oh, a beautiful bumble-bee. I was tearing along the High Street when I saw him down among the traffic; I thought he'd get trodden on — and he was such a beautiful, big, velvet fellow — so I took him up in my handkerchief. I don't know whether he liked it or not; he zoomed away there. But it would have been a pity to have let him get trodden on.'

I liked the eagerness with which he shared his little adventure. Turning, I asked smilingly: 'Are you a relation of St. Francis — friend of creatures ?'

'No,' he answered me, with little more understanding than the schoolboy, 'as a matter of fact, I haven't any truck with saints.'

'But,' I added persuasively, 'you have *some* relationship with St. Francis. You have a compassionate heart — you have saved the life of Brother Bumble-bee.'

16

Some Words Change

There is no telling what a reporter's first question will be when one comes off a plane. Crossing the tarmac for the lounge — burdened with overnight bag, reading-matter, coat, camera and umbrella — the question awaiting me on landing in England, was: 'What is your favourite indoor-sport?' Taken aback a little, I replied as smartly, and perhaps even as surprisingly: '*Conversation!*' One pair of eye-brows went up.

Some people claim, I know, that today conversation is dying out, that language, set against the rush and racket of our day, has almost ceased to be the main means of communication. Question this claim, and they start blaming the media — radios, transistors, and television-sets. The moment the family gets up in the morning, or comes in at night tired at the workingday's end, there is a scramble to get meals — and noise to accompany that scramble. And often — the meal over — for the rest of the evening, a volume of sound over-rides conversation, because it's a lot less effort. A neighbour can pop in — it makes no difference; or a long-time friend call — the pattern of the evening is set. An hour or so later, each will go out through the same door, without having shared a thing close to his or her heart.

This seems to be one of the contributions to the wide-spread loneliness that we know today, one of the saddest manifestations of our modern life. For there is nothing we know of as human-beings, to take the place of conversation — it lifts us up above the pets we keep, and animals of the fields.

I visited a friend's building-area, to see a new house almost completed, and was shown 'a conversation-pit' — a lowered floor in the lounge, somewhat like a large, low seat before the heater. I'd never seen an arrangement of the sort before; and I found myself wondering about it. Good conversation, to me, came rather like the wind — blowing where it listeth, not knowing rightly whither it came, nor whither it went. It proclaimed itself a miracle — at heart, it was a giving and taking, a sharing and withholding of words and eloquent silences. It was far removed from any organised setting, much less was it a competitive exercise in which the last person to draw breath was counted the winner. (The statistics, I believe, for those who like to make an art of a delight so artless, claim that the average speaker's daily word-flow reaches twenty-thousand!) Maybe! But surely we are not much concerned with statistics here. 'Once in a while', says one, 'when doors are closed and curtains drawn on a group of free spirits the miracle happens.' Friends do not require that a specific number of words be spoken, or that silences be interspersed: the fascinating thing is how often, when one takes the lead, it becomes plain that all have been thinking along similar lines; time gets lost in timelessness, words become princes that were slaves before, and enrichment is the result. But it can't be engineered. It would be a thousand pities if this matchless experience should for music, noise, radio, T.V., or any other reason, die out. Conversation is compounded of three essential qualities — self-giving, sincerity, and warmth-of-heart — that might all be covered in the attractive quality of a mountain woman, of whom it was said: 'She was born interested!'

It's a golden thing! Among the most meaningful passages of the New Testament are those recording our Lord's conversations. A rabbi, of course, in those times, often walked with his disciples, conversing as they went; and we have snatches of such between Jesus and His disciples. I think of their journey through the corn-field; their talk as they came down from the Mount of Transfiguration; and there was that famous conversation with the woman at the well, who came to draw water at mid-day, because other people wouldn't talk to her, or talked about her. Then there was little despised Zacchaeus, called down out of a roadside tree, to receive Jesus as guest under his own roof. A wonderful setting for conversation that was! O. Henry the story-teller, nearer our own day, talked about 'injecting a few raisins of conversation into the tasteless dough of existence'; but there was nothing of the kind about any of those occasions. They were each too real, too human to be doughy! And the same can be said of Nicodemus, the shy ruler, meeting Jesus in conversation on the roof-top at night, the winds stirring. The record we have of that out-door conversation shows it as one of our Master's most revealing hours. Along with it, one must put that wonderful indoor conversation toward the end of His life as He sat in the Upper Room with His friends. And there must not be for-gotten that conversation with the two down-hearted men — though Dr. Leslie Weatherhead thinks they may well have been man and wife, making the journey back to little Emmaus, and home, a few miles from Jerusalem. Joined by One other they walked into the setting-sun — and that piece of road, under those circumstances, was to feature in one of the most wonderful conversations in the world. It ended in a modest meal together, recognition of their Companion, and an instant return over the miles to Jerusalem to share that conversation! 'Did not our hearts burn within us,' were their words, 'while He talked with us by the way!'

A blessed experience, 'conversation', eagerly, revealingly shared!

*　　　*　　　*

But the word is used differently in many other places in Scrip-ture; I was at first perplexed by it. Happily, the scholars came to my aid. In instances they gave, they assured me that the word '*conversation*' carried a much more embracing meaning — 'a person's conduct, behaviour' — derived from the Latin *conversari*. 'Only let your conversation be as it becometh the gospel of Christ,' (Philippians 1: 27) is a case in point — meaning much more than words shared; translated more to our understanding by the Revised Standard Version: 'Only let *your manner of life* be worthy of the gospel of Christ.'

(And suddenly, 'a shaft of sunlight' burst upon my understanding of this word that, used over and over in the Epistles,
had perplexed me often.)

But now, so many of the Bible words have changed — which
is the soundest reason why we need new versions all the time.
Not only have there been remarkable archeological discoveries — old scrolls, manuscripts and treasures — confirming passages long known, or throwing new light on them;
but words themselves in which we have read of such things,
have changed.

The most obvious, as we turn the pages of the beloved
Authorised Version, 'the best words in the best order during
the best period of our language', are the archaic pronouns,
'*thou*', '*thy*', '*thine*', and the verb endings '*est*', '*edst*', '*eth*' and
'*th*', and the now obsolete '*whatsoever*', '*howbeit*', '*peradven-
ture*', and so forth. But these are not all: more than three
hundred words have changed their meaning since 1611 —
words like '*comprehend*' for 'overcome', and '*quick*' for life,
not for 'speed' as we use it today in our mania for car-transport,
and jet-travel. In Psalm 124: 3, where the Psalmist, full of
gratitude, recounts a wonderful deliverance from some who
would have 'swallowed us up quick', he means those who would
have 'swallowed us up alive'. '*Comfort*' is another word
commonly met with in Scripture. 'In the New Testament', Dr.
William Barclay reminds us, 'it is used to mean far more than
soothing sympathy.' Always it is true to its root meaning —
for it's root is the Latin '*fortis*', meaning 'brave'. The Christian
comfort is the comfort which brings courage. Paul talks about
'The God of comfort who comforteth us in all our tribulation
that we may be able to comfort them which are in trouble with
the comfort wherewith we ourselves are comforted of God.
Francis Asbury, the father of the American Methodist Church,
used the word in its original sense, in his *Journal* — though it
reads quaintly now: 'Our conference ended on Friday,'
said he, 'with a *comfortable* intercession.' And noting the change
in the word, we know now what he meant in 1774. and it is
something that no strong man need be ashamed of. '*Cunning*'
is another word that has come to have a different meaning in
our day. We meet it in modern thrillers. The Psalmist cried:
'If I forget thee, O Jerusalem, let my right hand forget her

cunning' (Psalm 137: 5). And his word translated 'cunning'
was the good, honest word for 'skill'. '*Prevent*' is another word
that has puzzled many a one, unfamiliar with its ancient
meaning. We know what is required when we are called to
'prevent' a matter; but in the century in which the Authorised
Version was translated, it meant simply 'to go before, to clear
the way of difficulties, to prepare for the one following'.
The servant of a prince or travelling nobleman did this —
he 'prevented' his master, so that on arrival, all was in readiness.
The word still appears in the beautiful English Collect —
and properly understood, is full of meaning: '*Prevent* us, O
Lord, in all our doing with Thy most gracious favour.'

Lately, when a husband, within my hearing, confessed to his
wife that there were too many words in the Bible that he didn't
understand, her immediate answer was: 'Silly muggins, get
yourself a new translation — there are any number of them to
be had. The R.S.V. is my choice.'

Words live — even Bible words — and change, like all
other forms of life; so there is no possibility of translating a
book into modern language once and for all.

Ideally, one needs to have at least two versions at hand —
the Authorised for its long-time associations, its solemn
majesty and beauty; and a more recent translation, for its
handling of the modern language that you and I speak in our
most responsible moments.

*   *   *

A letter awaited me in London one morning, It was from
a Commander at Morden College — *another example of
how words change* — for it has nothing to do with studies.
My subsequent visit showed it to be a beautiful home for aged
merchants, with a hospital and chapel, and gardens.

Soon, sharing tea with the Commander, I was listening to
the story of the Little Merchant of Aleppo. John Morden was
a goldsmith's son living in London, in the seventeenth century.
Above anything, he loved ships, and whenever he had leisure,
he found his way down to the Thames to see the tall-masted
ships that came up the river. 'One day,' he told himself, 'I'll
have one of my own, and sail to strange lands, and buy beautiful
things!' And that day came. He got three ships with tall masts

against the sky, and plenty of room below to stow beautiful things. With his heart full of dreams, he sailed away to the Mediterranean, and made his way to Aleppo, the great trading-centre of Syria.

There he bought bales of silks, quantities of sweet spices, and a collection of crafted treasures. He became rich. But after a number of years away, he began to long for London. Unable to wait, he made his way there — whilst his three little ships were loading — 'I will be there to receive them, on arrival,' he said. 'As ever then, I shall reap the rich reward of their trading.'

It was good to be back in London; but days passed, without sign or sight of his little ships. Meanwhile — wanting employment — John Morden hired himself to a gentleman as a servant. Bereft of his ships, he was soon poor.

One day, waiting upon his master, he chanced to overhear a snatch of conversation which made his heart race. Three ships, it was said — three ships from the East — had arrived in the River Thames. After so long a wait, John Morden could hardly allow himself hope. But the moment he was free, he flung on his coat and hat, and ran to see what truth there was in the rumour.

Certainly there were three ships in; but were they his? Soon he knew; they were his three ships! And overcome, he fell on his knees, and vowed to God there and then, that he would do something to help other merchants who might fall on difficult days. With the rich reward of his three ships' trading, he chose a piece of land near the River, and with the best architect of his time, built at Blackheath, Morden College.

And forty-five men live there today, including the Commander who invited me to tea!

17

Easter Days

Whenever I have shared a chicken-dinner, and been invited to 'pull the wish-bone', my secret wish has always been the same — to see spring come in the English countryside, just once more. There's nothing like it. My little poem: 'Repeat Performance' sets out to say as much:

This drama of delight never stales —
is no rumour, lovely lie;
Spring's sunshine finds the snow
impatient to be water,
the crocus to don her golden gown,
branch and leaf to speak their lines again.

A repeat performance, it is still unsurpassed —
Summer's leafy luxury.
waiting in the wings.

[R.F.S.]

Good Friday morning – part of this miracle of New Life — found my steps, with those of my friend, turned towards the oldest church on a London street. We had already been inside this fine Norman building — but this was Good Friday. And we had come with others, expressly to worship, not to look about us. Already we had heard the story of little Rahere the King's jester, who, to keep a vow made in a time of sickness, had drained the horse-market site of Smithfield — then the Smoothfield — and founded the church and hospital on this spot. We had actually helped St. Bart's — St. Bartholomew's Hospital — with a street-collection day, and had later stood beside the little jester's tomb in this wonderful old church of St. Bartholomew the Great. The finest view of the interior, we had been assured, was from under the organ gallery looking east; better even than the western vista through the massive Norman columns to the choir.

In relatively modern times, encroachments which defaced it had been removed, and the beautiful, ancient building restored. (The Lady Chapel had been used for commercial purposes; no less a journeyman-printer than Benjamin Franklin, had served part of his time there. Its last tenant had been a fringe manufacturer. For a time, there had been a smithy in the north transept, and the cloisters had been long used as stables. The crypt, during the same grievous times of defacement, had become a wine cellar in part, the remainder, a coal-cellar. On the positive side, it was claimed that Tyndale was ordained in St. Bartholomew's; Hogarth was baptised there; and that both John Wesley, and David Livingstone worshipped within.)

At the close of the Good Friday morning worship, in which we were privileged to share, the Rector and choir led the congregation out into the thin spring sunshine of the church-yard, to observe a quaint annual ceremony which provides for twenty-one aged widows to pick up sixpence each from a certain flat-topped tombstone. The little ceremony went back — the Rector assured me later, in reply to my letter, when he said he wished I had made myself known — to the endowment of Mr. Joshua Butterworth, a law publisher, who gave £22 10s. od. in Consols, the interest from which provided 6d. for each of the poor widows on Good Friday, in perpetuity, and a distribution of hot-cross buns.

But the emphasis on change that we had sensed inside, now caught up with us outside. For in the Parish it was no longer possible to find the stipulated number of poor widows eligible for the charity. (Like the latter part of the story of change within, this was a good thing. Many who sing the old hymn with the words 'change and decay' in all the world endlessly associate the two — but they don't need to be associated.) The same could not be said of the monetary worth of a shining sixpence in our day — that had changed too, and very greatly. Two widows, with adequate claims, stood by that morning, as the little ceremony went forward — for the rest, junior members of the congregation, and a number of adults like

Rene and myself, who accepted the Rector's invitation, finished up the buns.

But there was *no change* in the reality of Good Friday itself — it went deep down to match the need in human hearts, though, as we were aware, changes in our way of thinking were constantly taking place. It was inevitable that from generation to generation, changes should occur, especially in this twentieth century. (Though we are sometimes a little deceived; there was no need to go further than the modern passion for luxuriant hair. Away back as far as 1560, during the reign of the First Queen Elizabeth, it was decreed that 'No Scholler doe weare any long lockes of heyre uppon his heade, but that he be polled, notted, or rounded after the accustomed manner of the gravest Schollers of the Universities under payne of 6s. 8d.' Changes are often superficial, though that of sixpence, or six-and-eight-pence real enough. We talk about 'winds of change' — and in a score of ways, we find ourselves as little able to do anything with them, as to change the habits of the elements.)

The disciplines of sociology and psychology, can help us here, to respond with a certain amount of pliability — even in our religious life in the Church. Life once was centred in a more parochial experience around the parish church, the village, or much more slowly-moving town where everyone knew everyone; where men went out to work, and women stayed at home, unless they were servants, cooks, governesses, nurse-maids. Then came war — and even within great London, as G. K. Chesterton observed there day by day, undreamed-of changes occurred — the men to the fighting, the women to the factories; their young daughters to the professions, hitherto unopened to them. To use his words: 'Twenty-million young women' — who up till now, had been dependent on their fathers' bounty — 'rose to their feet with the cry, "We will not be dictated to", and proceeded to become stenographers!' Home-life, in many places, had to take on a new pattern. And inevitably, Church-life has been affected by this change in social and domestic environment. The Church's vitality, some tell us, depends on its ability to respond to this — but I think it depends for its vitality on something far deeper. (This is not to under-rate a realistic pliability — in every realm, life teaches us the need for that. And we men and women of Faith have to go on learning.)

But despite what change can come, we are based on a tremendous certainty that the first Christians lacked *on the first Good Friday* — and had to wait for, on Easter Day. The Risen Christ! *Between Good Friday — that could then never have been called 'Good' — and Easter Day, this world experienced most deeply, its greatest possible change.* It put wings on the feet of the down-hearted, laggard disciples, and a message on their lips:

They told it,
not in some safe, distant place
where nobody had yet heard —
but in that very city
where men had shouted hoarsely,
'*Crucify Him! Crucify Him!*'

They told it,
not after weeks, years,
when passions had cooled —
but at once, within Pilate's hearing,
and of all who judged, soldiered, shouted,
involved in that dastardly deed.

They told it,
confidently believing —
ran, meeting their living Lord in the way —
a personal confrontation
that more than an empty tomb reported,
changed the world!

[R.F.S.]

18

A Birthday in London

Travel-experiences are in this book — as is fitting — but I don't intend that it should be a 'travel-book'. To write such successfully, these days when so many travel, one ought to have circled the earth hopping on one foot, or to have sailed its seven seas on a tin tray. I have done neither, though I have travelled extensively.

And I was fortunate enough to have reached London again in time for an old friend's hundredth birthday. Named after the Commissioner of Works, Sir Benjamin Hall, the B.B.C. had carried his voice to me clearly on the other side of the world. Standing some three-hundred-and-sixteen feet up — the great clock beside him, with its minute-hands fourteen feet long, and hour-hands nine feet — he had faithfully marked the hours. When a test was made, the margin of error was no more than two-tenths of a second! On more than one New Year's Eve, I have stood on the midnight pavement beneath Big Ben, to welcome in the New Year.

And on my old friend's birthday morning, I made my way on foot to Whitechapel Foundry, his birthplace. Crossing the threshold there, I came upon a kindly member of staff, ready to tell me of the great bell, its weight thirteen tons, two hundredweight and three-quarters, and fifteen pounds. 'The first Big Ben,' said he, 'was actually cast in Yorkshire, and sent down to London by water. But the voyage proved rough, and the boat itself all but sank. When the unpacking was done in Palace Yard, the great bell was found to be defective. The only thing was to break it up, and re-melt the metal, and make an altogether new one. And the task,' he added proudly, 'came to us.'

Whitechapel Foundry, the steady voice at my elbow went on to tell me, had been casting bells longer than any other firm in the world. Its street-front, as I approached, appeared like a Cruickshank illustration of a Dickens' story — its own story not one whit less interesting, now that I had stepped over its threshold. The old building had been an Inn. Just inside I spied glass cases with models and moulds, flanked by framed pictures of bell-casting. 'We were on this spot in 1638,' said my kindly guide, 'though actually the Foundry started across the road as early as 1570.'

With that piece of information, we moved from the tiny office, to the yard, with its earthen floor, and box of flowers growing below a window. The story all sounded so familiar — covering so much honourable service — that it allowed of no ostentation. 'In the early part of the Reign of the First Queen Elizabeth, Robert Mot began making bells here in White-chapel. And some of them,' added my guide, 'are still speaking out. In time, Mot was succeeded by a kinsman.' (I liked his way of compassing history, making it so vivid.)

Passing through the tiny yard, I all but stumbled against a number of finished bells, up-turned there. One by one, I learned their story.

Upstairs, we came on several men busy at their benches, fashioning hand-bells. Some were concerned with their early rough shape, some with fitting clappers, others with their tuning. 'Let me introduce Ern Oliver,' said my companion. 'His family has been connected with Whitechapel Foundry for just on two hundred and fifty years.' That craftsman was busy testing the pitch of a hand-bell. We shook hands. 'I have a sister in your country,' were his first words, on learning where I came from. 'In Auckland — quite a big city, I think.' 'Yes,' I could reply, with some astonishment, 'I come from there!' 'In the long story of bell-casting,' I found myself adding, after we left Ern's bench, 'you must now have bells in many parts of the world.' 'Yes, we have,' came the answer. 'Whitechapel bells are now ringing all the way from Aklavik in the Arctic Circle, to New Zealand, your country, through Australia, Africa, India, the Indies, China, Russia, and the Continent of Europe!'

Downstairs once more, we found the workmen about to break off for lunch. Immediately in front of us was an immense furnace — looking like an early Bible-illustrator's idea of Hell.

Beside it, lay twin heaps of metal. 'You may know,' explained my kindly guide, 'that bells are made from part copper and tin. Here you see this material waiting. When the furnace is "apped", as we say, the molten metal is run off into a ladle, and after skimming, is poured into its mould.' Speaking to me as non-technically as possible, he had nevertheless, to mention the 'core' and the 'cope', and the inscription each bell would carry, and the secret of its tuning.

From the days of the First Queen Elizabeth, to the present reign of our beloved Second Elizabeth, seemed a long span of time — as indeed, the last crowded hundred years, the life-time of my old friend, seemed that June day.

*   *   *

Paul Hentzer — a traveller interested in bells four centuries before me — is remembered for a famous saying: 'The English are vastly fond of great noises, such as the ringing of bells.' For myself, I admit to emotion when from a distance, across the countryside, their mellow tones reach my ears. Closer, I have several times climbed into bell-ringers' towers. I believe there are still fifty-thousand bell-ringers in England, with about eighty-thousand bells!

One old story passed on, is of a parishioner who desired to leave money in his Will, to install a bell in the parish church — but with the doubtful proviso that 'it need not be in tune, so long as it prove loud, and could be heard afar'. One thing is certain to me, his request would never have met with favour — least of all in Whitechapel Foundry. With rare craftsman-ship, and care, Britain has earned her name, 'The ringing Isle!'

*   *   *

A day later — the sun westering, work coming to a close for many — I made my way down Fleet Street to the Strand, again on foot, since that is the best way to know London. In what light remained for chance discoveries, my eyes came on a building, offering the name of a firm, and beneath, the proud words: *By Appointment to Her Majesty Elizabeth II, shirt-makers'*. And in a trice, I was covering the long centuries once more! Very domestic! But, of course, as mother of a household, including father and sons, Her Majesty, would need shirts, as she needed other things — carriages, clocks, coffee, and the rest — though I had never thought of it before. Finding that 'By Appointment' sign gave me pleasure, and set me to following up this particular line of Royal service.

The first craftsman, outside the Court itself, to receive such an honour, was a little clock-maker, Thomas Herbert. Back in 1692! He was honoured with an order 'to make a large pendulum clock going thirty hours, with a chain, to be carried with His Majesty in a coach, and six alarm-watches for six pages of His Majesty's Bed-chamber'. He fulfilled that Royal order, 'By Appointment', and was granted, a handsome parchment bearing the Royal Coat of Arms, to show his honour.

Following this line of interest, I discovered that today, about a thousand belong to the Royal Warrant Holders' Association. Some time ago, they were visited by 'The Lady of the House', to mark the Diamond Jubilee of the Association. Special craftsmen and tradesmen from all over the kingdom were invited to London's Guild-hall.

Among those eligible, I was interested to mark-out Walter Gamble. Unlike the Royal shirt-makers, he did not fasten his 'By Royal Appointment' sign on the front of his premises, but on his van — since he was responsible for sweeping the Royal chimneys at Windsor Castle. And that must be a considerable task! Another unusual holder of the honour, is John Weatherstone of Glasgow — the Queen's bag-pipe maker! And there is the Queen's Muffin-man — an honour first given to old Mr Edward Tong, at seventy-five. So good were his wares, that they appeared regularly from his bake-house; and when the Royal family of muffin-eaters were not at Buckingham Palace, supplies were dispatched to Windsor Castle, or Sandringham.

Long ago, I discovered, Reverend William Bell of Elswick was granted the official title, 'The King's Preacher'. He was allowed to display the Royal Coat of Arms over his church-porch, proclaiming that he preached, 'By Appointment'. (Paul, apostle of the first Christian century, would have been interested in this. He claimed something even greater, for himself. '*I am appointed a preacher*, and an apostle, and a teacher' [2 Timothy 1: 11]. It never entered his head to carry a plaque, or an inscribed parchment to prove it — but then he received his 'Royal Appointment' from Christ, the Lord of his life's service!) There is a sense — and very real it is — by which every Christian preacher today, preaches 'By Royal Appointment'. Nor does it end there — every Christian worker, man or woman, whatever his task, her task, may claim as much. Charles Wesley saw this clearly — and stated it as clearly in a simple petition:

Son of the Carpenter, receive
This humble work of mine;
Worth to my meanest labour give,
By joining it to Thine!

19

Beauty Abroad

Do you ever find yourself puzzling: 'What makes a city beautiful, apart from its architecture?' I suppose there are as many answers, as there are people to whom one might address this query. Somewhere in the prosaic service of London Transport is a poet who helped me to my own answer one day. I had never met him, and had no idea of his name. But on my way to a business appointment under an overcast sky, I paused, as before 'a shaft of sunlight', to copy down his words on a poster: 'Leaves rust on the trees. The distant hills are smoky blue against the sky. Already the yellow stubble is scarred by the plough, and the wind and the winter rain send the rich autumn colours back to the earth. This is the time of year to walk in the woods . . .'

This was a reminder of common, natural beauty, which is always changeful beauty. 'There are certain unhappy individuals', Geoffrey Fletcher tells us, in *The London Nobody*

Knows, 'who take no pleasure in London. Such are frightened by its immensity, a magnitude that emphasises the emptiness of the heart. The city is too big for them, a mere desert of bricks and mortar. Or else they are dwellers in dormitory areas, dull grey commuters concerned with buying and selling, typing pools and paperwork.' Routine tasks have to be done, of course; but it was, I think, because of the very pressures on me that day, that the inmost secret of the poet's words came to me. The year was closing in, but there was still beauty to be had — the beauty of autumn. Perhaps this is a discovery of maturity — not one that young people easily make. The city, at any rate, owes much, I am certain, to those who keep themselves everywhere on the *qui vive* of expectation. If they can't go to the woods at the weekend, they can walk in the park nearest — and London is surprisingly rich in parks — if they can't rejoice in blue sky over the South Downs, there is sky over Westminster and the river beneath.

To get a glint of colour in a great city is as refreshing as to come upon 'a saint in Caesar's household'. It took me hours at first, to shake off the depression that settled on my spirit between Tilbury Docks and London. Stewards on that occasion, trundled my bags up the gang-way, and transferred them to the waiting train. And the following man-made waste of houses, little backyards, dismal and limited, with their dreary lines of washing, followed me till my eyes lightened on the soot-blackened station of St. Pancras. But this was only the first hour of my first visit. The city has its drab spots, but it has much else. Suddenly, I saw St. Paul's firmly in my line of vision, and the trees of a park un-named; next I was fascinated by the 'never-ceasing torrents of the Strand'.

Soon, I learned, that nothing so characterised the city as her plane trees. East and West End, nothing discourages planes — tall buildings, built-up areas, factories or soot. They march along the Mall from Admiralty Arch to Buckingham Palace — trees of rich and poor. Nobody mistakes them — harlequins among trees — with bark in places flaking off in the early autumn, leaving great yellow patches.

Had the Psalmist lived in London, instead of where he did, he could never have been satisfied to lift up his heart to God, as he did, crying: 'Thou hast made summer and winter!' In declaiming the delights of those two seasons, he probably felt that he had been daring enough. For there was an old belief amongst his people that rival deities were responsible for these extremes. The contrasts they showed, it was claimed, were proof of mutual enmity. As the god of summer had a mind to cheer, the god of winter aimed to curse with short days and bitter cold. The climate the Psalmist knew best was one of contrast. But greatly daring, he declared that his God, the Supreme Creator, *made both* — the warm, murmurous days of summer, and the dark, grey lifeless days of winter. And we are grateful that he coupled the two seasons — but, as far as I am now concerned, the story is not told without a word about the beauty inbetween — the riot of russet and gold!

It might have been ordered that we should gather nuts, and fill barns without any such overflow — but that was not God's way. 'Beauty in Creation,' I heard Dr. H. H. Farmer say, 'is the overflow of God's heart; it is the unstudied Divine word uttered, apparently, for no particular purpose . . . an unnecessary, delightful superfluity; therefore more eloquent of the Divine mind than almost anything else.'

Laurence Houseman, in a letter to Dick Sheppard which I came upon, wrote: 'An elm *turning yellow* before my eyes across the meadow is one of the most beautiful things I have met since my return from abroad, and says more to me about the real character and processes of God than many sermons.'

One of my memorable jaunts out of the city in autumn, was to Burnham Beeches. Some trees had been lopped, so that they grew in odd, gargoyle shapes; but to see the late afternoon sun filter through their gold in long, slender shafts, and to walk inches deep through the rustle of gold beneath one's feet, was to carry away a lasting sense of the beautiful generosity of God.

* * *

A greater number of my fellow-guests, I discovered, went in search of beauty of another kind. To that end, it was only necessary to step into a great London store, and peruse a list, and dial a number belonging to a particular preparation to be had in jars, in slender tubes, or in boxes. To save any awkwardness, a phone was provided, unattended, and the service was free. Of course, I must not undervalue this — in the presence of Him Who clothed all Nature in beauty, the contour of the countryside, the rib and shape of each single leaf, I could not do that.

* * *

But when I have said this, I am still persuaded that His greatest beauty abides somewhere else — in the secret places of the human heart and spirit.

I came across a strong hint of this in an East End Mission where I went to help a little. The first day I entered that throbbing centre, I was shown around in company of another making her first call. Unexpectedly, we came upon the kindergarten in session. Seated were a hundred or more tiny ones — tiny Cockney children. 'But look at the size of them!', exclaimed my companion — and turning to the one in charge: 'Whatever can you teach them?' For answer, she said, after an eloquent pause: 'Well, first we teach them to wash their hands, and to blow their noses — and then to associate all beautiful things here, with God. After that, we tell them some New Testament stories!' And soon I saw that they did more than that — there was great beauty in that place, that drab setting — there was the beauty of tenderness, of laughter, of fun.

* * *

The beauty of consideration for one's fellows, I kept on finding in the City. One example was a friend's discovery — but she sent me to share it, as she shared generously many forms of beauty. 'Few I have talked with so far seem to know it's there. You'll have no difficulty — you'll find it easily — it's on the edge of the pavement near Green Park.'

And I did. This find that I'll never forget, was The Porters' Rest — a well-worn wooden bar across two metal legs, shoulder high. The inscription it bore made plain its origin and use: 'On the suggestion of R. S. Slaney, Esq. who for 26 years represented Shrewsbury in Parliament, this porters' rest was erected in 1861, by the vestry of Hanover Square, for the benefit of porters and others carrying burdens.'

That said a great deal about the beauty of compassion. The more so, as far as I was concerned, since on my way to London,

that time, I had come through India, and had been introduced
to a *soomai tangi*, 'a burden bearer'. Fashioned of a thin slab
of stone across two uprights, it took no imagination to realise
what a God-send it would be in that exacting climate. (Later, I
learned that an altar had been erected in the new chapel at
St. Christopher's Training College, in Madras — in the form
of a *soomai tangi*! What could be more fitting than that one
should recall at worship, the compassionate words of the Lord
of worship? 'Come unto Me, all ye labouring and *burdened* . . .'
(Matthew 11:28, Moffatt.) Those who thought of worship as a
burden in itself, hadn't sensed the reality of it.) Few, if any of
us, travel far in life without carrying a burden — it is part
of the human condition. So it is wonderful, when at any level
of meaning, one can lay down one's burden momentarily, and
by faith, catch one's breath, and straighten one's shoulders
before going on. We need our 'porters' rests' — as now I
think of our one-day-in-seven for worship!

*   *   *

Another within the great city who showed this same beauty of
compassion, was none other than 'Saint Guy' — as a Cockney
mother mis-called him, in pointing out his figure that stands
in the courtyard of the great hospital he founded. Actually
'Saint Guy' was far from being a conventional saint — he
was book-seller, miser, gambler, and philanthropist. But in
his heart was this God-stirred beauty. His gifts, it is claimed,
'rivalled the endowments of kings'. Ian Nairn — in his recent
Penguin paperback guide that I chanced to pick up — says
wonderingly: 'The figure of Guy leading a sick man into his
hospital is all compassion, without the least taint of moralising,
or the horrible smugness of Victorian charity . . .'

The great city has unending instances of the beauty of God,
for one's eyes — and one's heart!

20

Aunts As They Are

It is just as well, perhaps, that I cannot identify the person who dared to ask: 'Are maiden-aunts human beings?' For I am one myself.

There was a time when to admit as much took rare courage — but it's not so now.

When first I looked into the matter, I was surprised to find uncles mentioned in the Bible — but not aunts. What seemed at first a ray of light, came to me when I learned that around 1611 — when the Authorised Version came out — the affectionate term for such a relation was *'mine naunt'*. It set me hunting again, but I searched in vain — the word was not there.

So I was driven to secular literature. My earliest find was from Sir Richard Steele, in the same century — and scheming families didn't show up too well. He wrote:

Miss Margery Bickerstaff, my great-aunt had a thousand pounds to her portion, which our family was desirous of keeping among themselves, and therefore used all possible means to turn her thought from marriage.

The method they took was, in any time of danger, to throw a new gown or petticoat in her way. When she was about twenty-five years of age, she fell in love with a man of agreeable temper and equal fortune, and would certainly have married him, had not my grandfather, Sir Jacob, dressed her up in a suit of flowered satin; upon which she set so immoderate a value upon herself, that the lover was condemned and discarded. In the fortieth year of her age. she was again smitten; but very luckily transferred her passion to a tippet, which was presented to her by another relation who was in the plot. This, with a white sarsenet hood, kept her safe in the family until fifty. About sixty, which generally produces a kind of latter spring in amorous constitutions, my Aunt Margery had again a colt's tooth in her head; and would certainly have eloped from the mansion-house, had not her brother Simon, who was a wise man and a scholar, advised to dress her in cherry-coloured ribbons, which was the only expedient that could have been found out by the wit of man to preserve the thousand pounds in our family, part of which I enjoy at this time.

Still, in the same century, I find Viscount Irwin writing to his wife: 'My pretty dear Penny. I wonder whate diversion you can find at Baraby among my olde ants who are as mannolcolly as the Devill?' Poor old aunts! What could they do? It was no joke being a maiden-aunt in those days!

But times have changed, and any number of us these days, find ourselves happily fulfilled in marriage, or in a professional life. One hasn't to defend oneself against the charge of being a prudish personality. Once, a perfectly attractive maiden-aunt — with, or without a thousand pounds, and interfering relations — had to spend many of her days in a straight-backed chair between an aspidistra and a handsome tea-service, a tapestry panel of her own stitching on the wall. Her life consisted mostly in supporting Mamma; on her special days, when leaving cards, callers came for tea and a tinkle of conversation. With a little luck, she might get out sometimes, to pay calls herself. Outside of Church-hours — and still within the parish — she might visit the sick and lesser-folk socially, with a little basket of goodies. From time to time in company — corseted tightly, as was the fashion of the time — she might suddenly 'faint away', on some slight emotion. The stuffy air in the parlour was, at times, enough to achieve this noticeable feat.

Between 1809 and 1894 — all that long time afterwards — Oliver Wendell Holmes was still writing:

My Aunt! My poor Aunt!
  Her hair is almost grey;
Why will she train that winter curl
  In such a spring-like way?'

Why had he need to ask? No aunt today would so much as allow the use of that word 'poor'. She had now a wider choice than ever aspidistras, tea and hand-work provided, or the later chance to go into another woman's home as a maid, or governess. Even with what little had been added with the years, she could seldom relax over a demure game of croquet; or admit herself 'crossed in love'. Conversation with the opposite sex, to say nothing more, was so restricted, and properly guarded.

In *The Girls' Own Paper* of 1880 — greatly daring — appeared a notice of work being offered women clerks in an insurance office. But it began: 'The young ladies employed by this company must be daughters of professional men, clergymen, doctors, officers in the army, navy, merchant and of similar social grade.' That drew a strong line against many. Then it went on:

Their hours are from ten in the morning till five in the evening, with an hour between one and two for luncheon. Luncheon is provided in the building — and well provided, too — at the exact sum which it costs. When it is over [and this is a precious addition] there is time left for a walk. On the streets? Oh, no, on the roof. The roof has been fitted up as a promenade for the young ladies. The salary begins at 32 pounds a year and rises by stages of 10 pounds ... [But there was one additional point:] A considerable number of young men are employed in the office of which we have been giving an account, but with them the young ladies never come into personal communication. So far as meeting is concerned, they might be a hundred miles apart, the two divisions of clerks even coming into the building by separate entrances.

This way, a young unmarried woman was denied the privilege of ordering her own affairs — if it wasn't scheming relations, it was scheming employers!

Yet there were some, I must report — including young people — who actually thought of their aunts as 'human beings'. There was young Gibbon — who later became famous as the author of *The Decline and Fall of the Roman Empire*. Of his aunt he wrote words that none of us following on ought to forget. 'If there are any who rejoice that I live, to that dear and excellent woman they must hold themselves indebted. To my aunt's kind lessons I ascribe my early and invincible love of reading.'

Aunt Jane Austen was another. The highest ambition Jane's brothers and sister could pass on to their young, was that they should 'endeavour to resemble dear Aunt Jane'. After her death, the record assures us 'the nieces and nephews did not care to come to Chawton'. Their dearly-loved aunt who encouraged them in their reading, and other delights, was no longer there.

These we know of; but we can only surmise there were others, of whom as much might have been said — but they were in the background, if anywhere, and I have not heard of them.

In time, the First World War broke over social-acceptances, and un-guessed changes resulted. Some maiden-aunts took charge of service-clubs — adding to their modest experience, all manner of exciting exploits. Some turned to the professions, and were accepted. And it wasn't long before single women had won for themselves a place they have never surrendered. Till now, many offices would be in a sorry plight, if relieved of their services. Margery Fry puts the issue clearly: 'Better eliminate the directors,' says she, 'than remove "our Miss Smith" who knows all about everything, and where the papers about the Uruguyan order of last month will be found. No! Those who undervalue the unmarried woman,' says she, 'must think again'!

Apart from the professions, good causes in the community would sag, if not die overnight, without the consecrated care of the unmarried.

*   *   *

When my friend, Rene, and I hiked around southern England, with our haversacks, we came to the Shrine of Saint Catherine. Wearing stout low-heeled shoes, I am sure we would have looked to Gibbon, and to the young fry who clustered around Jane Austen, unbelievably emancipated. Which, of course, we were!

On the way, we chanced on two other bachelor-women, carrying haversacks, approaching the same wooded area of Milton Abbey. And with a chuckle between us, we went on

together. The Chapel — with its thick walls and Norman
doorways, was a reminder that Saint Catherine of Alexandra
was credited with miraculous powers, as the *patron Saint of
Spinsters*. And she must have been one of the busiest saints in
her day, since there was so small a chance for any girl who
sought her, if 'she failed to get her man'.

Light-heartedly, we set down our haversacks, and together
read through an old prayer-rhyme, composed by one with a
pretty turn of phrase and a desperate urgency:

> St. Catherine, St. Catherine,
> O lend me thine aid,
> And grant that I never
> May die an old maid.
> A husband, St. Catherine,
> A *good* one, St. Catherine,
> But arn-a-one better than
> Narn-a-one, St. Catherine,
> *Sweet*, St. Catherine,
> *Handsome*, St. Catherine,
> *Rich*, St. Catherine,
> *Soon*, St. Catherine.

Each of us — I hadn't any doubt — had come to the cross-
roads of choice with a prayer on her lips, but judging from my
own experience, it wasn't this one. Contradict me, if you care
to!

21

Guidance As We Go

As I waited on the wide Welsh roadside, commanding a view
falling down into a valley, a bus drew up. In a moment, those
who poured out of it were singing; they were members of a
choir, going to a festival. And *Cym Rhondda* never sounded

better than there — though its opening words perplexed me, as ever: '*Guide me*, O Thou great Jehovah.'

It had a comfortable churchy feeling — but what was it saying? Could God really guide individuals? Or was it just proclaiming a sort of general reality, as Arthur Mee, the popular editor of our day, seemed to be content with? 'We know,' were his words, 'that there is something not ourselves that comes with us through the years, which gives us strength in weakness, courage in failure, endurance in long suffering, and the assurance that, whatever may befall, our destiny is secure. He guides us, and the bird, along our pathless way, and in His good time we shall arrive.'

'Comfortable, yes — but is it enough? I am more than a bird,' — I am a human being, part of the highest of God's creation. I keep coming to moments of choice; I have days when things press upon me, when my natural powers of consideration don't seem enough.'

Countless others beside myself, of course, have queried the opening words of William Williams' Welsh hymn. Nor does enlightenment always come easily, nor all at once — but to me, it did presently come, as 'a shaft of sunlight'. I have learned to know it in a wider sense since.

Any, grown-up in the Christian way of life, I believe, can expect God's guidance to come through Bible-reading, worship, and prayer, if spiritually alert. I am now able to recount various experiences of this — though not all have happened in Church, the most likely place.

But God guides one often, I find, within the ordinary affairs of life, mingling with others — He guides me often *through those others*. Mildred Cable, with whom I talked in London, and later, on our side of the world, set me thinking like this. At the last oasis before she set out into the Gobi Desert, she found herself faced with the vastness of it. When she admitted trepidation to her camel-driver, he replied: 'But *other people* have crossed and left tracks. And at night-time, there will be stars. Have no fear; rest your heart, lady; there will be a way.' That is how God guides each of us through people — in friendship, Christian-fellowship, the reading of a biography, an autobiography, even a well-written novel. No one of us is ever the first to pass this way!

Then God may choose to guide us one by one, *through the shining gift of reason*. It would be a mistake to ask Him to save one the bother of thinking, of weighing up the *pros* and *cons* of a possible line of action, of using common-sense. 'God,' says Dean Matthews of St. Paul's, 'does not put the right ideas into our heads, but if we are in communion with Him, He purifies our minds and motives so that we are able to arrive at the right ideas through the faculties which He has given us. Some people seem to suppose that if they say a prayer and then make their minds a blank, the first notion that occurs to them is the guidance of the Spirit. This I believe, is dangerous nonsense. We have to use our minds and think as we can.'

Often, God guides one *through one's conscience*. This is not to make the mistake of calling it 'the voice of God', because at times it is not — as Paul's conscience was mistaken when he set himself to persecuting the Christians, believing he was doing God a service. Conscience, mistaken, can slander one's neighbour, can tell a 'blue' story for popularity's sake — it's finer edge dimmed, even shameful.

There are times when God guides one *through one's emotions* — one's love, pity, indignation. It might be a moving missionary story; an account of a crippled child; a refugee blasted by war-conditions; or a mother starving. One may be guided to give a pound or two, to offer one's nursing qualifications, or one's skills at a craft.

Responding to God's guidance, coming in any of these ways, life is enriched. The prayer: '*Guide me, O Thou great Jehovah*', is well expressed in *Cwm Rhondda*.

* * *

I can't recall anyone who had to learn this more pointedly in our day than Amy Wilson Carmichael. She was born with soft brown eyes. Her mother's eyes were blue — and loving her mother — little Amy wished she had blue eyes, too. Blue of skies, blue of seas, blue of the soft, distant hills of Ireland where she lived, seemed to her the loveliest colour in the world. She thought about her eyes a lot; and one night when she crawled into bed, she remembered that her mother had said that God could do anything, if only one prayed with faith, and a loving heart.

And that night when the light was out, before she snuggled down with the comfortable sheets under her chin, she prayed. She told God that of all the colours, she liked blue the best; and since He was so wonderful that He could do anything, would He please change her brown eyes for blue ones? Content — her prayer finished — she then snuggled down, and went to sleep. First thing, in the morning early, she scrambled out of her bed. Pushing a chair over to the old chest-of-drawers where was a looking-glass, she looked into it — *and her eyes were still brown!*

She could hardly believe it. Disappointed and puzzled, great tear-drops began to well up. Hadn't God taken any notice? But, of course. He must have. Mother had said that no matter how little anyone was, a sincere prayer would always be answered. But she still had brown eyes! Then suddenly, as she tried to puzzle it out, a little question jumped into her mind: 'Isn't *No* an answer?'

And she never forgot that morning. Ever afterwards, when she wanted a thing very badly, and prayed, she was always careful to ask God to answer according to His will. And He did that. So sometimes, of course, He had to say '*No!*'

When she was grown-up, Amy Wilson Carmichael wanted very much to go to China, as a missionary. She prayed for God's guidance. But God, the loving Father, had something very much better for her, so He had to say '*No*'! And He guided her, not in so many words, but in circumstances — though she had all her things packed ready in two tin boxes. When presently, the doctor examined her to see if she was fit for such an undertaking, he had to say that in all honesty, he couldn't give her a pass. And she never got to China.

Then she tried as hard to get to Japan — but that wasn't the best and happiest thing either. After a year there, she had to return home. She had to learn that when one asked for guidance, sometimes the answer had to be '*No!*', sometimes '*Wait!*', sometimes '*Yes!*'

Eventually, she reached that happy day. Instead of going to China or Japan, she was able to go to India — and there she stayed for over fifty years, at a particular missionary job, gathering little orphan children about her, the happiest family anywhere. She never had any doubt that she had been guided aright. The thousand little children she gathered at Dohnavur, were so happy. And she dressed them all in blue to match the skies and the seas and the soft blue hills, though they all had brown eyes that perfectly matched her own!

22

Temptations at Hand

Travelling with friends can be fun, but travelling alone in one's own small car can hold advantages. Driving north to Scotland, I suddenly found myself approaching Ecclefechan, birth-place and burial-place of Thomas Carlyle. For years the name Ecclefechan had fascinated me; but I'd never before had a chance to stop-off. And the next hour passed all too quickly.

Chatting upstairs, I found myself sharing the story of an earlier caretaker — and chuckling over it. A certain visitor, as he came to leave, it seemed, paused to express his thanks for the pleasure his visit had given him, and to confess that the time had proved all too short — he could have spent hours among the books and letters displayed. 'Yes,' had answered the old caretaker, 'I know what you mean. Many a good hour I've spent reading those words myself, when I should have been working.' And then she had added: 'I haven't much time now; so when I come up here to dust, *I just leave my specs downstairs*.'

Pondering that piece of village wisdom as I journeyed on, it seemed to me the most sensible thing I'd heard about handling temptation — and we all have to handle it. Opportunity, they say, calls seldom; but temptation is always at the door. Though it is not often a choice between bad and good: much more often it's between good and less good.

The petition in the Lord's Prayer is often on our lips, but how many are clear about what they really mean by 'Lead us not into temptation'? A modern version puts it: 'Bring us not to the test.' But even that is vague; for as metal is tested in engineering, by external stresses and strains, so are we men and women, by life — not to make us fail, but to prove our resources. My good Scottish friend, Dr. William Barclay, I remembered, had put it strikingly: 'Temptation is not so much the penalty of being a man — it is the glory of being a man.' A few days after Ecclefechan, I learned through the National Bible Society of Scotland, that this puzzling petition of the Lord's Prayer had been erroneously rendered for the Republic of Liberia — not, the equal of 'Lead us not into temptation', but 'Do not catch us when we sin.' Laughable!

Nevertheless, it does need making plain, that *temptation in itself is not sin*. That truth came as 'a shaft of sunlight' to me when first I saw it. And I found proof of it in the fact that Jesus, our Lord, knew temptation — though He was without sin. When the Bible says: 'He was tempted in all points like as we are', it is not saying that it was worthless — it is saying that He found it as real as we find it, and that it came to Him on the level of most natural, plausible concerns. 'Whenever I am about to commit any folly', Scott makes one of his characters, Bucklaw, say, 'the devil persuades me it is the most necessary, gallant, gentleman-like thing on earth, and I'm up to saddle-girths in the bog before I see that the ground is soft.' That's how temptation mostly meets us, isn't it? It was that way with our Lord.

His first temptation in the Wilderness was to turn stones into bread, to match His natural hunger. The desert about Him was littered with rounded lumps of lime-stone — very like the loaves He used to eat, from His mother's baking. Every man, He told Himself, had an honest right to eat. He was about God's business — and how could He do that if short of strength? It was as natural as that — and He had the power to change stones into bread. It all sounded reasonable enough like your temptations and mine mostly do. But He suddenly saw it for what it was — the temptation to use His God-given powers selfishly for His own ends.

Soon came a second temptation — and as plausible. In a vision, it seemed, He was raised to the pinnacle of the Temple, and invited to prove to men God's power — to cast Himself down, assured that God would under-gird Him. That way, it was suggested, men would be won by the spectacle. How better could men see God's power proved? But dazzling men's minds, Jesus knew, was not God's way of winning devoted allegiance. That way, He would be called on to produce ever greater and greater sensations to hold them. And the Kingdom of God, He knew full well, could not be built on any such basis. 'You must not put the Lord your God to the test', were words from the Old Testament which rang in His ears; allegiance won by sensational action, cannot embrace heart, mind and will, as the Kingdom of God requires.

The third temptation was as plausible — to win for God the whole world of men in one fell swoop. Above all, He wanted to win men. But how? 'Fall down and worship me,' said the tempter, 'and I will give you all the kingdoms of the world.' But this was world-leadership on the Devil's terms — even if he possessed the power to do it, which, of course, he did not. It was a wholesale sovereignty, outside God's purpose — having no regard for men's free-will, given by God Himself.

Clearly, our Lord wanted His disciples to take into account these three dramatic temptations of His, and the subtlety of them — for He told of them Himself, since there was no one else present who could have told of them.

Nor were they all — any more than your temptations and mine, can be got over early in life. Not at all. Towards the end of His life, our Lord turned to His disciples with these revealing words: 'Ye are they which have continued with Me in My temptations.' So there were others besides those three in the Wilderness.

Temptation — or 'testing', to use the more generally acceptable word — is an inescapable human experience. But there is no sin in it. Temptation is part of the battle of being human; that is what those words mean: 'He was tempted like as we are!' 'Count it all joy,' says the Apostle James, 'when you fall into divers temptations', and again: 'Blessed is the man that endureth temptation: for when he is tried, he shall receive the crown of life which the Lord hath promised to them that love Him.' 'Put on the whole armour of God,' says Paul, 'that ye may be able to stand against the wiles of the devil.' Says John Wesley: 'Leave no unguarded place, no weakness of the soul.' 'Walk on the other side of the street', the little child who delighted Kenneth Graham, would have said — sharing in her own small way, the *same priceless secret of avoidance* that Ecclefechan gave me. Speaking of her: 'I know what she wants most,' said Harold. 'She wants that set of tea-things in the top shop window, with the red and blue flowers on 'em; she's wanted it for months, 'cos her dolls are getting big enough to have real afternoon-tea, and she wants it so badly *that she won't walk that side of the street when we go into town*. But it costs five shillings.' Deliberate *avoidance* is a telling secret in handling temptation. If you have to watch your weight in adolescence, don't work in a sweet-shop; if you know full well your weak-spot, avoid the area in which it lurks!

When temptation actually descends, you and I have each the same resources as had Christ; God is never unresponsive.

23

An 'Amen' by Heart

A friend drove me out from Ilkley, in a round-about-way, to Haworth, the one-time home of the Brontës. We came near to losing our way, and had to alter our direction — which reminded me of the delightful story of the lady of 'culture-vulture aspirations', making her first visit. She quite lost her way, and at the bottom of the hill, had to ask help of a man working nearby: 'Tell me my good man, is this the way to Brontëland?' To this, looking up, he replied calmly: 'Ee, ah doant know, missus, ah cum fra Haworth meself!'

The little town is dour enough, struggling up the steeply-rising side of a valley. At the top is the tower of the church, seen from afar, on the edge of the wild, empty moors. The High Street, in all essentials, unchanged since the Reverend

Patrick Brontë himself arrived to minister in 1820. The parsonage — in which every one of the Brontë novels was written — remains much as when the family lived in it. Nearby is the Black Bull Inn, to which the frail authors' reprobate brother made all too many visits. And out beyond the expressionless windows staring, is the expanse of old gravestones, each with its tragic story. (Now, the old house — once so very private — is opened on occasion to people like myself, interested in the improbable story that it holds.)

There, Emily's rose-wood desk still stands; the lamp by whose meagre light *Jane Eyre* was written for the outside world; together with Charlotte's piano and work-basket. The latter interested me especially — together with the collection of tiny manuscripts — written on minute home-made notebooks, stitched through, of a size that could be easily whisked out of sight into a work-basket on the lap, should a step be heard, or a door be opened.

It is all but unbelievable that in such a dour setting, ministering to the demands of an austere father, not counting those laid upon them by an irresolute brother, anything of lasting literary worth could be accomplished. Yet so it was — despite also frail health, and serious sickness. The brief tragedy of their lives is recorded in the church register — one by one, with the exception of Anne, who died at Scarborough, they all died here, and were buried within sight of those staring windows. Charlotte — who won greatest fame for her *Jane Eyre*, *The Professor*, *Shirley* and *Villette*, died in 1855, at thirty-eight. And none of the others even reached that early age: Emily, born in 1818, died in 1848, author of *Wuthering Heights*, and a goodly number of poems; while Anne, author of *The Tenant of Wildfell Hall* and *Agnes Grey*, died at twenty-nine; and brother Branwell, at only thirty-one.

Divided between drink, and drugs, and an attraction for a woman older than himself, his record was a grievous one. 'He made,' as one put on record, 'the days heavy with anxiety, and the nights hideous with brutal revelry. Once, at least, in one of his wild outbreaks, he set fire to the rectory.'

At last, a Sunday morning came, when he died. A crony associated with The Black Bull Inn, slipped out of his room, just before his family entered, as the bells began to ring for

Morning Prayer. Branwell's old father fell to his knees there beside his bed. And when he finished praying — to everyone's surprise and pain, as Charlotte later recorded, Branwell himself was heard to add 'Amen!' Charlotte never forgot that happening. 'I myself', said she, 'with painful, mournful joy, heard him praying softly in his dying moment; and to the last prayer which my father offered at his bedside, he added "Amen". *How unusual that word appeared on his lips, those who did not know him, cannot conceive.*'

Poor Charlotte! She understood what that common word meant, how rich it was — being far from a decent word of termination. And on her brother's lips it seemed all wrong, since for years he had done nothing but scoff at religion. There had been in his way of life nothing in the least related to the good, glad things of God. And now it was too late.

The word in its Hebrew, meant '*so be it*' — spoken or sung; it was a word of *splendid assent*. (Some time before I made my way to Haworth, this fact clearly struck me as 'a shaft of sunlight', to make all the difference to my own rather thoughtless use of it at the close of prayer, and at the close of worship. I had just never thought about it much.) In the olden days — as in the Psalms 41: 13, and 106: 48—it had been accompanied by the rubrical direction: 'Blessed be the Lord God of Israel from everlasting to everlasting: and let all the people say "Amen!"' From synagogue, it had gradually passed into the liturgical use of Christian congregations — and so down to us. St. Jerome used to say of the early Christian community, that the 'Amen' that followed the prayers was like a clap of thunder. And, in time, it summed-up the phrase continually on the lips of the good Saint Francis de Sales: '*Yes, Father! — Yes! and always Yes!*' A word of splendid assent! Martin Luther wrote to his friend Melancthon: 'I pray for you, I have prayed, and I will pray, and I have no doubt I shall be heard, *for I feel the 'Amen' in my heart.*' This was not a word to be lightly uttered — it carried, when properly understood, the assent of all one's faculties. It was this lack in her brother's use of it, that so pained Charlotte in that shaded room that Sunday morning.

(I shall always remember how Sir Walford Davies, Master of the King's Musick, Gresham Professor of Music in the City of London, taught me to properly sing 'Amen!' I attended a lecture by him; and stresssing the use of this word, he said unforgettably that night: 'The *Amen* can't be too good!')

*   *   *

The Brontës were more sensitive than most of us. But there is no escaping the ebb and flow of a sensitive spirit, by any one of us, any more than sunny skies, and clouds that veil the sun. 'I like people who have continually the same temperament,' said a twelve-year-old in my hearing. But by this time he will have become an adult himself, and will have learned the impossibility of full life that way. We know what he meant — but even if it were possible, how very dull it would be!

But there is all the difference between *moods* and *moodiness*. When I first saw this plainly, it was as 'a shaft of sunlight' to me. Moods are meant to change, even as a sail to winds that cross one's steady course. Moodiness, far from natural intermittences, suggests a lack of control, a radical weakness.

Even those saints, whose memorial I saw in the street in Oxford, Latimer and his fellow-martyr, Ridley, knew this. Said Latimer: 'Pardon me and pray for me, I say. For I am sometimes so fearful, that I could creep into a mouse-hole.' That from a great spirit who could give his life for his faith!

Dr. Benjamin Jowett, distinguished theologian, and Master of Balliol, nearer our own day, said much the same: 'I wish you wouldn't think I am such a saint. You seem to imagine that I have no ups and downs, but just a level and lofty stretch.'

But life isn't like that. Some, of course, have a constitutional tendency to look on the *down* side, rather than the *up* — though one should never accept any mood as permanent. Others lack physical fitness, and this affects one's view of life. The tides of response flow most naturally in a body tingling with health. One has a duty, personal, immediate, and widespread, to keep one's body, mind and spirit fit. This is not to forget that there is a world of difference between *moods* and *moodiness*.

24

Things Unchanged

One morning, I popped out of bed and pulled up the blind for a peep at the weather. Just then the alarm shrilled, for I had to make a train-journey that day.

I had no idea, of course, of the privilege that awaited me in Manchester, in addition to addressing a packed audience in the Free Trade Hall. But when I arrived early in the day, at that famous domain of the Hallé Orchestra, I was granted the use of Sir John Barbarolli's sanctum for relaxation, between my obligations during that crowded day and night.

Sir John, of course, came from a long line of music-makers. His father, Lorenzo, was a first violinist in the orchestra of La Scala, Milan. In those days life had not been easy. The family, as time went by, moved to Paris; then to London. The years there gave young John time to grow up. Most of them were spent in Leicester Square, at the Alhambra, the Empire, and the Queen's. A little orchestra in a hotel restaurant and grill-room must have seemed at times very unexciting; but there was one thing that thrilled me, as I occupied Sir John's room, off-and-on, that day. He remembered his father saying: '*A. is A. and a quaver is a quaver wherever it is played!*' What he was saying was: 'There are some things forever stable, amid all the changes life can bring.'

I didn't mention it to anyone with whom I had to do, but that profound truth sustained my spirit that day. What I had to offer that vast audience, in serious utterance, and in laugh-provoking incident, I knew, was something more than a handful of experiences, a heartful of ideas — it was a Person: '*Jesus Christ, the same yesterday, today, and forever.*' Between the *agrarian* life, as men had known it once, and our *techno-urban* civilisation today, was a great gap; but this great fact stood. Of the God Who sent Him to earth — and to Whom He witnessed — Dr. William Temple of our day could say: 'When we deliberate, He reigns; when we decide wisely, He reigns; when we decide foolishly, He reigns; when we serve Him in humble loyalty, He reigns; when we serve Him self-assertively, *He reigns!*'

*   *   *

After Manchester, the busy weeks of lecturing flew by — till I was called to Liverpool, to join my ship for Canada, *en route* for home. I had no obligations in that great city; but I promised myself I would take adequate time to see the Cathedral. And what an experience!

My discovery that the distinguished architect of that great new building, to the glory of God — Sir Giles Gilbert Scott, O.M. — was also the designer of *the country's smallest, the telephone kiosk*, added a new dimension to my approach, and to my understanding of the New Testament challenge: 'He that is faithful in that which is least, is faithful also in much.'

Threading my way on foot up to the Cathedral, I was struck by its solid beauty and strength. It stood, with its immense tower in warm-red stone. Entering, its spaciousness — without any pillars to obstruct, compact and unified around its tower — moved me by its grace, conducive to worship.

The Dean and Chapter, very wisely, I learned, had set their hearts on the worthiness of memorials to be admitted. One in that beautifully uncluttered atmosphere, I shall never forget — the chastely-lettered inscription to the memory of the world's great helper of crippled children. It read: 'Here rest in honour all that could die of a pioneer of orthopaedia, Sir Robert Jones, Baronet, January 14th, 1933, aged 74 years.' *All that could die*. I came away repeating those simple words over and over.

Whereas cathedrals are usually the outcome of many designers and builders — reaching over years, even centuries — Liverpool owed its beautiful wholeness to its being the work of one growing mind.

Its Lady Chapel, with windows set to the memory of noble women, was the first part of the whole which Sir Giles built. Grace Darling, long one of my heroines, was there; and Charlotte Stanley, gallant defender of Lathom House, representing another kind of courage; Elizabeth Fry, of prison reform;

and Agnes Jones, fittingly enough one whom Florence Nightingale sent to Liverpool to effect changes in Poor Law Institution Nursing; but the one before which I paused longest, was that to Kitty Wilkinson, a humble woman belonging to Liverpool. Her tribute read: 'Indefatigable and self-sacrificing, she was the widow's friend, the support of the orphan, the fearless and unwearied nurse of the sick, the originator of baths ...' It was for this last service to the poor, that I knew her name.

Kitty's little house had long stood in a mean Liverpool street — her door constantly open to those in need. This was particularly so when the dread cholera struck the city.

She was fortunate to have a small well of clear water; and she was not slow to see that a lack of personal cleanliness encouraged the spread of the plague. She invited her neighbours to use her own small wash-house. But much more was needed; and Kitty made her way to the authorities. To provide public baths and wash-houses for the poor, seemed to them a bold idea. But they gave it thought, and in time, established the *very first* in any city in the land.

Never will I forget that moment, when in the Lady Chapel, I found among the 'saints', *the Saint of the Soap-suds!*

*   *   *

I have often thought what a fine thing it would be if we could remember locally in our places of worship, others serving as humbly. In the quietness, remembering my own church — I wrote the following 'Beatitudes':

Blessed is that minister who finds his people daily translating his preaching into the bright prose of living; he shall preach well;

Blessed is the choir that clearly enunciates its words; the musical, as well as the hard-of-hearing shall share their praise;

Blessed are the lay-preachers who — knowing themselves not as able as the minister — yet hold themselves in readiness to fill a gap; joy shall be theirs;

Blessed are the women who do the flowers — in bare winter, as in blossoming summer; their love of beauty silently praises God;

Blessed are the church-cleaners who work weekly when nobody is looking; their emphasis on cleanliness supports godliness;

Blessed is the youth-leader who stirs to get a full complement of teachers; after many years, he shall reap a rich reward;

Blessed are the young parents who bring their little ones — and don't forget soft toys, and the removal of noisy shoes; peace shall reign;

Blessed are those who write business-minutes for action — not just to be precious in themselves; God will occasionally perform miracles;

Blessed are the mothers given to fellowship, who visit the lonely, spread tables and cook to the glory of God; hungry hearts bless them;

Blessed are those who attend the prayer-group — remembering the burdens and joys of others; they shall be counted in heaven the salt of the earth;

Blessed are all who bring their minds as well as their feelings to worship; God shall rejoice in their wholeness, and shall be called their God, now and forever. Amen.

[R.F.S.]

*   *   *

Liverpool, at last, days behind, our ship pushed on through the mighty St. Lawrence River. I found strength in recalling that when Lord Tweedsmuir — John Buchan, and his Susan — served Canada as Governor and Lady, they lived on the banks of the St. Lawrence. Susan told how she sometimes lay awake at night, listening to the sounds that served as background. Two always sorted themselves out. First, there was the sound of the busy, aggressive little hooters, belonging to the tug-boats that pulled heavy barges up against the stream. But now and again — with the energetic little hooters — would come the tinkle of bells. She welcomed them. In time, she learned that they issued from a nunnery not far away; they called the nuns to prayer during the night-hours of darkness. And to Susan Tweedsmuir, they seemed strangely related, as she lay awake, happy to balance *the hooters of activity*, with *the bells of contemplation*.

Pondering on her words, as our boat pressed on, I wondered if her husband ever had similar thoughts. In his autobiography: *Memory Hold the Door* — one copy of his completed manuscript despatched from Canada only a fortnight before his death — he had written of his beloved parents: 'My father was a true son of *Mary*; my mother a daughter of *Martha*. Had she had his character, the household must have crashed, and if he had been like her, childhood would have been a less wonderful thing for all of us.'

Martha was represented by the hooters, Mary by the bells — the busy, practical energies over against contemplation and prayer — both of God's making, God's giving, not *contradictory*, beautifully *complementary*.

25

Places to Know

The cities of Quebec, Montreal and Toronto — about each of which I could write a book — offered me their delights, added to what friends could show in the surrounding country, wide corn-lands, stately mountains, snows and lakes at Banff, the winding way through the Rockies to other friends near the coast. In every day was some breath-taking beauty.

*   *   *

Eventually Canada's wide embrace had to be surrendered for the States. I was making a second visit to New York's canyoned streets, and cloud-loving towers. At night, I slept further from the earth than ever in my experience — and at greater cost; so that when I snicked out the light, I couldn't at once decide whether to go to sleep and enjoy it, or to stay awake and know that I was having it!

The first morning, Saturday, a pleasant stranger approached me, bearing a tray from a self-service counter I had discovered.

'Can I sit at your table?' she asked. We exchanged names, and professions. She had read several of my books — and as proof ran off their titles. She was a teacher, in the city to do a special course.

'Tomorrow is Sunday,' she broke into the conversation at an unlikely point. 'Can I take you to church? You've heard of our preacher, I'm sure — everyone has who reads — Dr. Vincent Peale. He makes you feel a *million d-a-ll-a-r-s!*'

I had to reply: 'Actually, I'd made up my mind to go back to Riverside Church, some distance off, where Dr. Harry Fosdick used to minister. I went there last time I was in New York. I know he isn't preaching there now, but I'd like to go. I grew up on Dr. Fosdick's books, *The Meaning of Prayer*, *The Meaning of Faith*, *Manhood of the Master*. (Later, I was to have the privilege of dedicating one of my own books to the Doctor: *High Business* — using one of his prayers for my title: 'Thou wilt do high business in our souls. Mould us, transform us, encourage us, inspire us, empower us.')

'That's O.K.' replied my newly-found friend. 'As it happens, I have my auto full of gas, at the Y.W.C.A. — we could do both — get to the Marble Church for the early service, and *come out in the last verse of the last hymn, and be in Riverside for the first verse of the first hymn.* The service times would just allow it.

And though it might not be the ideal approach to worship, that is what we did. The ground-floor was full as we entered Riverside, and we had to go up by lift, to gallery seats.

Dr. Fosdick I spotted below, as a member of that vast congregation. He, more than any other, I knew, had helped religion come alive for many there, and in retirement, they loved to have him with them. One would-be member I know of, had approached him during his ministry in the great church, saying shyly: 'I'm not even sure what I think about God, *but I should like to work out my spiritual faith inside the Christian fellowship — and not outside.*' Riverside was ready to meet such; and three years later, the same seeker after reality, came to the Doctor saying: 'No words can estimate what this has meant to me; each year, clearer insights, deeper assurance and life more and more worth while.'

No church, of course, was ever meant to be the mere gathering of the good and self-satisfied, the easily satisfied, ready to sign on the dotted-line of belief, and occupy a pew once a week. But 'the best way of knowing God', as one had said, 'is to frequent the company of His friends.' The solution of a problem is important; but the contagion of worshipping spirits, much more!

Riverside's lofty tower has long been a landmark in the life of many — symbolising rich values, in a 'thing-centred' world.

*   *   *

I am not by nature a lover of architectural heights; but in the case of New York's then tallest building in the world, I was able to reach its hundred-and-second floor by two lifts. And I'll never forget that. The sun was warming the famous Empire State Building with its last rays, going down in a miracle of lovely colour out beyond the Hudson River, Ocean liner-piers, and New Jersey. Beneath where I stood, the day's work was coming to an end for many. It was the moment when covers were being dragged over type-writers, desk-drawers slammed to, correspondence-files stowed away, hats and coats taken down from pegs.

I wondered how many of the thousands below were aware of the rare beauty of that moment. God was bringing another day to a close with effects that would never be quite the same ever again. Of His handiwork I had seen so much — the closing of many another day, gathered in to the cloak of darkness; mighty rivers, and unceasing seas; mountains girdling great prairies; Niagara, for which there are no adequate words; the colours of the Grand Canyon changing continually; the grave dignity of the *sequoia*. What beauty!

I had never been bluffed by mere size — even in America — but Sara Teasdale's words walked up and down in my mind, there as elsewhere:

Places I know come back to me like music,
Hush me and heal me, when I am very tired.

Beauty reaches one so deeply. Some forms of it, I know, can be accounted for as contributing to the on-going natural order — the colour and pattern of flowers designed to attract passing bees, and so secure fertilisation. But this theory has been over-worked from the start; and leaves out many of the

forms of beauty which have meant most to me — the sky at
sunset, as I saw it from that tallest building; the minute perfection of a creature from the bottom of a lake — unseen by
the natural eye — but beautiful beyond belief, when micro-
scopically examined; the shining spirit of a neighbour, faced
with a taxing choice; a fringe of graceful swaying grasses on the
edge of an otherwise denuded embankment. (There is ugliness,
of course, in shabby yards, in crowded sunless courts, in dark
places of ignorance where hatred, violence and illiteracy crouch.)

For all that, the Psalmist prayed when he looked abroad:
'*Let the beauty of the Lord our God be upon us*!' And still this
prayer rises to our lips, continually — where the end of day
asks us to pause; where men and women pledge life-long
love, and care for home-making; where leaders of the people
meet in conference to thrash out their disagreements, and in
justice, find peace; where craftsmen in woods and metals and
words and paint and music, pass on glimpsed eternal meanings
amid the pressing claims of Time.

Without this vision there is no reward in our going, without
this experience no satisfaction when twilight gathers us into
the night. We are made like this — in the image of God. The
Mass evokes such emotion in the devout Catholic; so also does
the pregnant quiet that the Quaker knows in his meeting-
house; and others of us find in shared singing of God's
praises!

True beauty is not only to be found abroad — as I know —
but I always feel a little embarrassed when the man at the
customs-counter asks me when I return, like this from across
Canada and the States: 'What have you got to declare?'

An air-queue struggling with passports,
more often than not, moves me to mercy;
and I don't bother the officer with all I'm
smuggling back — a bright coal of knowledge
picked up in a back-street book-shop;
a couple of sunny turrets from Quebec;
an arrow-head of homing birds at dusk
flying over Lake Ontario;
a tree in a Vancouver park, holding out
its arms to heal . . .

It's late, and he's tired,
and perhaps a little vexed —
though I could be mistaken about this —
for straightway I watch him take his chalk
and score my case, mumbling but one word, 'Next?'

[R.F.S.]

26

'Born to Belong'

It was wonderful to be home again. Many things continue to
change in 'this thin, brittle, mechanical life', to borrow Priest-
ley's words — but not this. *One is born to belong.* I remember
when I first saw this freshly, as 'a shaft of sunlight'. And it
reached out beyond family and home-setting. In the old
Book of Kings — for the most part full of battles and dastardly
deeds — I happened on the story close to my own heart. It
concerned one who shared many rich, royal blessings, far
from home. But a day came when 'Hadad said to Pharaoh,
"Let me depart that I may go to mine own country." Then
Pharaoh said, "But what hast thou lacked with me, that behold
thou seekest to go to thine own country?" (I can imagine the
pause at this point — the eloquent pause — Hadad's eyes on
the floor at his feet.) But there is no need to fall back on imagination — we have his little scrap of heart-history: *"Nothing"*,
said he, *"howbeit, let me go!"* Nothing he lacks, except — and
this is everything — *he doesn't belong!'* (1 Kings 11: 22).

'In the New Testament story of the Prodigal son,' I heard
my Epworth Press editor, Dr. Leslie Church, say in a broadcast over the B.B.C., 'there is that poignant moment when in
the famine-stricken land he struggled with the swine for
husks, "and no man gave unto him". No man could give
enough,' said my editor friend. 'It was something more than
food for the body he craved. At last, in that grim place of

haunting memories, he knows that he doesn't belong — and *where he does belong*. And his words are: "I will arise and go unto my Father, and will say unto him, Father . . ." '

The truth is — whoever we are, in riches or poverty — light dies out of our eyes when we have no sense of belonging. Some, in these days of the loosening of family-ties, the shattering of marriage-vows, the pressure of outside concerns once unknown, know it, to their sorrow — some all too early. After she had twice run away from a children's home — my newspaper reported with some pain — a little child from a broken home, gave her modern reason, in the mood of Hadad, and the prodigal: she was 'looking for *someone to belong to*'.

Poor little kid! She had no right to find being a human being so painful, so early. Rootlessness is a bad characteristic of our day. Dr. Paul Tournier, from the midst of it, in his book *A Place for you* — and what a striking title — says 'every man needs to *know he belongs*, that he has an identity, a place in life as a person.' This is not something that a psychiatrist has thought up, since he must say something to people who come to his clinic — something to help fill his book, as I use it now in mine — but not because I haven't lots of other things to say. It is a reality deeply implanted in the human heart; it was here from the beginning — long before Hadad, even; and it will be a reality even when you and I have gone upon our way.

Nor does it end easily by one's own effort — even by a casual acknowledge of things spiritual, and an occasional attendance at worship. So deeply implanted is the need to belong, that a bewildering sense of isolation does not automatically drop away when one bows one's head in a pew. From a Church in Germany — though geography has really nothing to do with it — I lately copied this confession:

This is our poverty
That we *do not belong* to each other,
Nor serve one another,
We go each his own way
And do not care for our neighbour.
We pray Thee, O Lord,
Redeem us from this estrangement,

Redeem us out of this loneliness,
Deliver us from the sin that divides us,
Join us closely in true love.

[Anon]

Doctors, psychiatrists, social-workers all tell us the same thing — that loneliness is the greatest single hurt the human heart suffers. And nothing like an increased pension from the Welfare State can make any difference — the deeply rooted need is a spiritual reality that persons have talked of through the centuries; though it isn't something that the Church has thought up, for them to talk about. Not in the least! Canon Peter Green of Manchester puts it simply: 'There is no emotion so necessary to a true religion, nor any so fundamental to it, as *the sense of belonging to God.*'

To any who might think this just the sort of thing a preacher would say, there is the word of the agnostic anthropologist Malinowski:

> Religion fulfils a definite cultural function in every human society . . . If religion is indispensable to the integration of the community, just because it satisfies spiritual needs by giving man certain truths, and teaching him how to use these truths, then it is impossible to regard religion as trickery, as an 'opiate for the masses', as an invention of priests, capitalists, or any other servants of vested interest . . . *Religion binds the individual to the other members of his family, his clan, his tribe, and it keeps him in constant relation with the spiritual world.*

All around us all the time are many rootless, restless, lonely people. I confess I belong to the Church as an expression of the deepest realities in my life — not because I am a 'hanger-on', but because I am a *human being.* Our Lord matched a deep human need when He taught us to pray: '*Our* Father . . . *our* daily bread . . . *our* sins.' Upon this belonging, He built His Church. The Draft Catechism of the Church of Scotland states it well: 'The Church is the community of those on earth and in heaven who through Jesus Christ, are united in fellowship with God and with one another.'

Belonging is so basic — when word-loving observers today talk about people being 'de-personalised', this is what they mean. Unhappily, some of us do what we can to hide it — unaware that it is no more than a mark of being human.

*   *   *

Lately, under the title 'Pensioner', I drew this word-picture:

My old neighbour needs to know that she counts:
Sunday she goes to Church — and is reassured;
Thursday she goes to town —
climbing aboard a suburban bus, nine o'clock
till three, on a pensioner's pass.
five cents each way —
for a few hours in gloves, a film,
a look at the shops, a bit of lunch,
and the feeling of being in the flow of humanity,
leaning against the breeze at the crossings,
waiting for the street-lights to change —
then on.

My old neighbour stands straighter,
taller, on Sundays and Thursdays.

[R.F.S.]

27

Seven Welcome Words

Come in for a neighbourly chat, pay a social-call, betray an awkward shyness, or confess to a family anxiety, and the most likely seven words, seven days of the week, you will hear where I live, are '*Will you have a cup of tea?*' There is no least need to underline the fact that Katherine Mansfield was a New Zealander, since she exclaimed: 'Very beautiful, O God! is a blue teapot with two white cups attending!'

We cannot at this stage, be sure who brewed our first cup — it might have been a missionary's wife, a trader's wife, a pioneer settler's wife, full of sweet hospitality and loneliness. There ought to be a monument to her — monuments have been raised to many-a-one who has made a far less important contribution to life.

Happily, we know, and can honour, the first Englishwoman to offer a cup of *afternoon tea*, in her home-land, half-a-world away. She was the Duchess of Bedford. About a hundred and thirty years ago, she gathered about her in her private sitting-room, a little group of friends, and dispensed to them *tea with little cakes*. Between the mid-day meal and late dinner, she confessed, she experienced 'a sinking feeling'. And this was her sensible way of dealing with that dilemma. (She certainly ought to have a memorial. If I ever hear of you gathering contributions for the same, I'll send mine along. And I'm sure I won't be alone — if Dr. C. S. Lewis was a typical Englishman; for he said, tying two of life's delights together: 'You can't get a cup of tea large enough or a book long enough to suit me.')

Tea was early known in England; in the *Gazette* of September the 9th, 1658, which carried news of Oliver Cromwell's death, appeared the first known advertisement for its sale. It read: 'This excellent and by all Physicians approved drink called by the Chinese "Tcha", by other nations, "Tay" alias "Tea", is sold at the Sultanes Head, a cophee house in Sweeting's Rents by the Royal Exchange, London.' No price was given; but we can be sure that it was not cheap. One record put the price at £3 for sixteen ounces; and when the relative value of money is taken into account, the cost must be four or five times multiplied. Tea had, of course, to travel great distances from the East to reach the English tea-pot. (Excepting water, today tea is reckoned the very cheapest beverage; every day, those who give their interest to such things, claim that over eight hundred million cups are brewed.)

One of the most delightful half-hours I can look back on in London, was spent with Mr. Stephen H. Twining, M.B.E. in The House of Twining, 216 Strand, W.C.2 — historian of the business that has continued unbroken through twelve reigns, two hundred and fifty years. When I left, he kindly gave me a copy of his delightful book. From its dust-jacket I copy: 'The name of Twining is so closely linked with tea that one may be forgiven for saying "T" for Twining and Twining for Tea!' The tiny premises, are set between larger buildings, spread little wider, or higher than its one open doorway. Not even Hitler's bombs that fell there devastatingly, managed to oust the Twinings; repairs were made, and the business continued, embracing both tea and coffee now for many years. Mr. Twining, who kindly autographed his book, is a direct descendent of the founder — 'with these qualifications', to quote from his delightfully illustrated pages, 'probably the oldest tea and coffee merchants in Great Britain, perhaps in the world, and probably the oldest rate-payers in the City of Westminster'. ('It is said that by 1683 there were over two thousand coffee-houses in London alone. There was usually a "cover charge" of a penny and the coffee was sold at two-pence a dish. Incidentally, the word "tip" is reputed to have originated in coffee-houses. Nailed to the walls were boxes into which the patron who required especially good or rapid service would put money. Each box bore the words "to insure promptness", the initials spelling T.I.P.')

Tea, it seems, took some time to win through to its present popularity — partly, I expect, because it was so costly and so difficult to get. Stocks which reached England came by way of the Continent, and were smuggled in. Exhorbitant duties were levied — up to fifty per cent — three-parts of all the tea served for a long time being contraband. The flat beaches of East Anglia were ideal for landing goods from small boats. Unhappily for the enterprising smugglers of tea, heavily-indented foot-prints were likely to give the show away, till the in-coming tide could obliterate them. The way to get over the difficulty, was to pay a local to drive his flock of sheep over the foot-tracks left on the beach, and so destroy the evidence.

Old Parson Woodforde makes a touching entry in his famous Diary, which reads: 'Andrews the smuggler brought me this night about 11 o'clock a bagg of Hyson tea 6 pound weight. He frightened us a little by whistling under the parlour window just as we were going to bed.'

Mrs. Pepys, no less — wife of our most famous diarist — was actually seven years behind her husband in tasting tea, which gives an idea of its scarcity. In her case, it can hardly have been a matter of cost. She had a bad cold, and 'Mr. Pelling the Potticary's advice was a cup of steaming tea.' But there were many tea-drinkers with small idea of how it should be taken. Southey used to tell of an old lady who, serving her friends, ate the tea leaves, and threw the liquor away. When the result seemed to lack interest, they added butter and salt. Others, for the same reason, are known to have added boiled onions. (I can't blame them, though I can't imagine the result.)

The high cost of tea, and the difficulty in getting supplies, led also to wide-spread adulteration — 'smouch' made of the leaf of ash-trees, steeped or boiled in coppers with sheep dung, was a paying proposition. Little wonder that parsons preached against it, and politicians made eloquent and lengthy speeches. Cobbett, who showed such good sense about many things, called tea 'a destroyer of health, an enfeebler of the frame, an engenderer of misery in old age'. *Well!* Others, when the supply became better controlled, and the social habit won popularity, wrote to the papers about it. One delightful example is too good to pass by, without pausing to copy. Addressed to the lady Editress of a popular London journal, in 1774, the gentleman-writer begins:

Madam, as I look upon you to be a person who knows the world perfectly well, and has the happiness of her own sex very much at heart, I wonder you have never thought fit to throw some admonitions concerning the moderate use of tea, which, however innocent it may seem to those who practice it, is a kind of debauchery! Were the folly of wasting time and money in this manner confined only to the great who have enough of both and to spare it, it would not call for public reproof, but all degrees of women are afflicted by it, and the wife now looks upon her tea-chest and table and its implements to be as much hers by right of marriage as her wedding-ring.

But there were some leaders among the people, wiser by far — and John Wesley was one of them. He had his friend, the famous potter, Josiah Wedgwood, make him a beautiful tea-pot, with a Grace worked on it: 'Be present at our table,

Lord ... etc.' So he definitely thought of tea-drinking as no unholy thing; perhaps he saw what a part it could play in corrupted eighteenth-century morals, when the craze for gin-drinking cursed so many. Anyway, he supported the idea of Church-tea-meetings, which became with time, real centres of fellowship. Many of the chapels went so far as to have their own crockery specially made — marked with the name of their local 'society'. (I have in my possession one such cup-and-saucer, given me in recent years, when one of those early chapels was demolished. And I treasure it.) John Wesley's own tea-pot remains in his house in City Road, London, along with other of his possessions. Any visitor from any part of the world can now examine it — though it has lost its lid, since an American lady 'snicked it' as a souvenir.

But nobody has any hope of stealing from us the pleasure and fellowship of a good cup of tea!

*   *   *

Rene and I still chuckle about our effort to get tea one day when we were on a walk. We called at a small café. Rene approached a young man behind the counter, to give her order: 'Please, may I have two cups of tea — one with milk, one without.' At that, he looked a little mystified, and gave reply: 'But which one without?' Thinking he had not properly heard her, my friend repeated her request; only to get the same reply: 'But which one without?'

At that critical moment, a senior woman swept into sight, with: 'O leave it to me, Terence!' And with that we got our tea!

*   *   *

Tea is such an important part of hospitality — and hospitality, these days, such an important reality when loneliness is every-where abroad. Many medical-men, psychiatrists, social-workers today count loneliness as the most wide-spread sickness of the spirit from which folk suffer. Our Lord spoke about a 'cup of cold water, in His name'; had He lived in our country rather in Palestine, I am sure we would have had some words from Him about 'a good cup of tea'.

Peter's injunction to the people of the first-century Church carries over his Lord's spirit. Said he: '*Be hospitable* to each other, and never grudge it' (1 Peter 4: 9, Moffatt). Many were on the roads in those times — in many cases, hounded from place to place for their Faith. It must have been wonderful to come upon an open door in their need, to be received into an hospitable circle. 'In the ancient world,' as Dr. William Barclay reminds us, 'inns were filthy, ruinously expensive, and of low repute. The Greek had always a shrinking from hospitality for money. Inn-keeping seemed to him an unnatural affair.' No wonder hospitality was regarded as a sacred duty among Christians. The writer of The Hebrews was moved to say: 'Do not be forgetful to entertain strangers'; and the writer to Titus, wrote: 'Be a lover of hospitality'.

And those words have never been more timely than now. Hospitality is more than a chair drawn up — though it is that; more than eating and talking — though it can start there. At its best, it is a readiness to give of oneself. Tagore, in our day, gave thanks to God, that 'Thou hast made me known to friends whom I knew not. Thou hast given me seats in homes not my own. Thou hast brought the distant near and made a brother of the stranger'.

This is a shining, wonderful essential in our life — and how often it starts with the simple seven-fold question: 'Will you have a cup of tea?'

28

Walking in High Places

Occasionally, an awareness of my comfortable height — five foot seven and a half inches — is reduced. I am thinking of a superb experience, when my human height against the sky seemed insignificant. Along with Rene, and another, I carried a haversack on The Milford Track, long called 'The Finest Walk in the world', deep into our country's Fiordland.

Off and on, I fell to thinking of Ella Adams, the first girl to walk the Track. It must have been a hazardous undertaking in her day. There is a discoloured photograph extant, of an early party in grotesque clothing. Ella probably tramped in knicker-bockers, like some of the ladies in that picture, with stout boots laced half-way up her shins, gloves, and a jaunty little feather in her hat. Since the weather must have been as unaccountable then as now — three hundred inches rainfall in the year — and the essential bridges across the turbulent mountain streams, then nothing but a few stout logs thrown across, I'm sure that Ella well-deserved the honour of a tiny lake named after her, at the top of the mighty Mackinnon Pass. (We were to come upon it, up-lifted three thousand four hundred feet, close by the cairn commemorating the earlier exploits of Quinton Mackinnon himself, that colourful character, who first discovered, and crossed the Pass in 1888. Ella's father — Chief Surveyor for Otago — might well have found the Pass, had he not been engaged on other tasks in those pioneer days. One of his men had reported to him that he had seen 'three explorers come over early one morning'. These were black swans; and 'as birds generally fly over the lowest gaps in a range', said he, 'I should not be surprised if that is where the Pass is.')

Once before — twenty-five years earlier — Rene and I had hoped to walk The Track; but running a summer-camp for young people, I had tripped and sprained an ankle an hour before we broke camp. So it was off. The more eager, now, because of our long wait, we were on the Track — striding freely in our heavy boots and double woollen socks, scrambling over stream-beds, clambering up steep paths where the green garment of the forest gave way to scrubby vegetation, and wide-eyed little mountain flowers.

Fiordland, we found, lay so far south, that we had first to fly to Dunedin, then take a lengthy bus-ride to Lake Te Anau, jade-green, spread a hundred and thirty two square miles under the sky — the largest in the South Island. Parting with the bus, we parted also with our city-clothes and shoes, to don skirts and blouses and woollen jackets, with rain-coats and sticks and cameras to hand.

First came the launch trip to the far end of the Lake, where, as the day ended gloriously with colourful clouds piled high, we came to our first sleeping-place, Glade House, nestling beneath trees beside the river. A stillness lay over all. This was our introduction to the sublime mood of the mountains.

Next morning took us across the river by a bridge, and on to an easy way, that kept company with the winding river, beneath handsome beech trees, native ferns margining the track most of the way. Ten miles on we came to Pompolona Hut, in the narrows of the Clinton Canyon. Its amusing name, we learned, went back to Mackinnon himself, whose pompolonas (Italian pan-cakes) cooked here, were famous. On one occasion, legend says, he had to substitute candles for the fat he required; but since his candles were home-made from fresh mutton-fat, the outcome wasn't such a culinary disaster as it sounds.

Still, there was no least habitation on the whole Track, except for the Huts provided — we saw no one but ourselves. In the company of the noble trees, pools, small lakes and giggling streams, we had for company only native ferns, and where the trees gave way, clumps of native flowers. When streams had to be crossed, we were encouraged to plunge in boots and all.

Nine and a quarter miles from Pompolona Hut brought us to our highest point, and far-off, long-ranging views of unparalleled grandeur. Toiling, under full sun, our packs growing uncomfortable, we were spurred on by the promise of a cup of tea at the top — if, our guide was careful to qualify, there was no wind. The little hut there stood rather precariously — already it had been blown away a number of times. We were fortunate, and never did tea taste so good. Hopping around us outside the hut were a couple of comical native birds — keas — with a pink and grey parrot-like look, friendly, as if they were the true host and hostess of the tea-hut. One dare not leave one's haversack a moment untended, or they would be into it, ripping the canvas apart.

From the high point of the cairn, in glorious calm, we took the most dramatic photographs of the whole walk. Range after range folded into a pattern that drew our eyes down the way we had come — the river appearing now but a thin, winding thread. I never felt more physically insignificant, but nowhere more awed by the immense genius of the Creator!

By mid-afternoon, we were descending the muscle-straining zig-zag of the far side, to our next Huts. (Any of our company set on photographing the famous Sutherland Falls — nineteen hundred and four feet of foaming perfection — had need to hasten, beyond the Huts, before the direct, overhead light of mid-day left. I left my two friends to come on at leisure, and hastened ahead. It was well worth my effort — the glorious waters coming down into a green pool, before they ran away. At one time, the Sutherland Falls were known as 'the tallest Fall in the world'; but some spoil-sport found another, a little taller still, in South America, and our boast was at an end. But who needed to boast in the presence of this loveliness?

Night found us the welcome ease of Quinton Huts — choosing our bunks, slipping thankfully out of heavy wet boots, washing our woollen socks. At first, my slippered feet made me feel top-heavy, and I missed the balance of my haversack. After a good meal shared, our bunks called.

Sometime in the night — following sky-blue days, and mountain-air tingling with life — rain started to hammer on our tin roof. As if out of a determined spite, it rained all that night — and all the next day, and all the next night, and all the next day, hammering hard. We were now a closely-intermingled company, the Track-keepers also driven in for shelter, the rivers on either side of the Huts, overflowing a-torrent, shuttering us off from civilisation. The single telephone wire was down. No other party could join us, so the Huts-manager assured us — adding that he had provisions enough. Time passed.

On the Sunday morning, somebody somehow remembered what day it was, and made his way to the old piano in the common-room for a sing-song. Familiar hymn-tunes soon gathered in drowsers, readers, letter-writers. Somebody asked for 'The Lord's my Shepherd', to the tune Crimond. The pianist could not oblige, so Rene was brought to the stool. She had little more than started when, surprisingly, the kitchen-door opened, and out stalked someone we had never seen before — an old Track-keeper, who instantly joined in the singing, contributing his part in a good, strong voice. And when it was at an end, he as suddenly disappeared; we never saw him again. What memories, what early home or church training, we wondered, did that loved hymn awaken?

That evening, when the rain ceased, and a glorious light hung over the mountains, the Huts-manager suggested that if we could rise and breakfast early, next morning he could get us on the Track again by six o'clock. That would allow us to do the final thirteen miles by lunch-time, when a launch could pick us up at Sandfly Point, and take us up an arm of the fiord to Milford. Into wool socks, boots and haversacks again, we were all eager for any activity by now — and were soon on our way. The Track was muddy, and even awash in some places; but the morning was tingling high with blue-sky sunshine. The lush growing things smelled beautiful!

When we reached the Hostel at Milford — that was to be our point of dispersal — we met bus-loads of disgruntled tourists departing. They had been shut indoors during the whole of the storm, and seen nothing of Milfords' boasted majesty — and now it was time to go. In the last twenty-four hours, we were told, ten and a half inches of rain had fallen on their roof, before the gauge had over-flowed. How much fell on our tin roof in the mountains, no one will ever know. The Huts-manager confessed to us that he had never before had to keep a party for so long a stay. From the immense bastion of rock at the rear of the Hotel and Hostel at Milford, ethereal white ribbons of water — minute water-falls — were still floating down; and under the blue sky, the imposing form of Mitre Peak raised its head before us — seen so often on tourist posters, but never before by us in reality. I felt reckless with my camera — the colours so crisp and beautiful.

In time, a bus conveyed us through the awe-inspiring Homer Tunnel that bored through the mountains, and led us by glorious lake-side views, beneath great trees, back to the settlement of Te Anau, where we were able to claim our bags. We had completed the round-trip — a long-time dream, not mountaineers, but walkers. Words one had used long before came back to me as a shining truth: 'You never enjoy the world aright till the sea floweth in your veins, till you are clothed with the heavens, and crowned with the stars . . . *Till you can sing and rejoice and delight in God*, as misers do in gold, and kings in sceptres, you never enjoy the world.'

29

Music and Marriage

Refreshment of another lasting kind, came to me one night. As a long-time member of The Chamber Music Society, I found myself sitting receptive in the Hall.

The Stradivarius Trio — Swiss artists — were there; and produced for me the miracle moment. Along with Weber Giger, their pianist, they brought to those of us waiting, not merely what an expert called 'the most Mozartean of Beethoven's early chamber music, Quartet in E. Flat, opus 16, for piano and strings'.

This sublime beauty was expressed by superb instruments. There were three — made in the sixteenth and seventeenth century by the master, Stradivarius himself. Harry Goldenberg, the violinist played the 'Aura', dated 1715, one of the rare instruments in the world today. It came from the master's golden period of craftsmanship. The viola, played by Herman Friedrich, was even older — bearing the name 'Gustav Mahler', and fashioned in 1672. It was the most precious of the three instruments. The violin-cello, entrusted to Jean Paul Gueneaux — the 'Bonamy Bobree', dated 1717, belonged also to the master's richest period. Thanks to a generous Swiss collector, none of the three priceless instruments was locked away for safe-keeping, but together were loaned to the trio who made music for us, and made it with seemingly effortless mastery. What came to us was mellow, and full of song, of sweetness and nobility.

The old poem — credited to the master violin-maker, as he plied his calling — came alive for me in a fresh way:

When any master holds 'twixt hand and chin
A violin of mine, he will be glad
That Stradivari lived, made violins,
And made them of the best . . .

T–E

For while God gives them skill,
I give them instruments to play upon,
God using me to help Him . . .
If my hand slacked, I should rob God . . .

Between those lines — as I pondered them later — there
waited a challenge, since God, to this day, cannot work such a
miracle unless man plies his skill; cannot give some things to
our world unless someone thinks; cannot work His will
among the nations unless someone prays.

*   *   *

Music, even such music, of course, is more than instruments
— as marriage is more than moonlight.

In London, one day, Rene needed a dentist. We got an
address from the hostess of a Club we frequented, and set off
by way of Harley Street. With its world-specialists, it suddenly
occurred to us, that anyone practising in the vicinity might
require a fee well above our usual range — Wimpole Street,
was near to Harley Street.

I as suddenly felt sorry that I had not bothered to check
the number of Elizabeth Barrett's house. 'How silly!' I said,
'when we're in the locality!' Not even the play we had seen
earlier gave us the number: 'The Barretts of Wimpole Street.'
All we could do was to walk on, ticking off the numbers, till
we reached No. 50 — the address on the scrap of note-paper
we held.

So imagine our amazement — on reaching it — to find
above the door, one of those blue plaques London makes use of,
to mark historic sites. It told us that in that very house had
lived Elizabeth Barrett! (Now it was our dentist's.)

In its quiet waiting-room, on the other side of that handsome
door, I had plenty of time to go over the outline of that
wonderful love-story. It was incredible to think from that
very address, Elizabeth had crept out to her secret wedding
with Robert.

And sitting there, I was able to recall the sonnet that she
wrote to her beloved Robert:

How do I love thee? Let me count the
ways.

I love thee to the depth and breadth and height
My soul can reach, when feeling out of sight
For the ends of Being and ideal Grace.
I love thee to the level of every day's
Most quiet need, by sun and candle-light.
I love thee freely, as men strive for right;
I love thee purely, as they turn from praise.
I love thee with the passion put to use
In my old griefs, and with my childhood's faith.
I love thee with a love I seemed to lose
With my lost saints — I love thee with the
      breath,
Smiles, tears, of all my life — and, if God
      choose,
I shall but love thee better after death.

Beautifully coupled within those words are *love* and *loyalty*. Love might reasonably express itself in the bursting glory of an hour, touching 'the depth and breadth and height' of one's being; but it reaches God-likeness only when it continues with the 'level of every day's most quiet need'. God has declared Himself in the dual qualities, as 'the Eternal, a God . . . rich in *love* and *loyalty*' (Exodus 34: 6, Moffatt).

'The poetry of words,' claims Oliver Wendell Holmes, 'is quite as beautiful as that of sentences.' If he means words like 'love' and 'loyalty', I agree!

30

Doubting our Doubts

Some people are proud of their doubts, and some people are ashamed of them. Others try to stifle them, drive them from the conscious to the subconscious. I remember when it dawned upon me as blissfully as 'a shaft of sunlight', *that doubts are as natural as growing-pains*. Actually, Dr. James Hastings described them in those very words: 'the growing pains of the soul'. Anyone who gets to middle-age without them, can fairly be said to be suffering from 'Peter-panism'. He is not growing. It would be strange to live in this age of science, with its cold wars, sputniks, and rising nationalisms, without growing-pains. It is easy to make a joke of it, as Evelyn Waugh does in the case of Prendergast, in *Decline and Fall*. But it is no laughing matter — neither, of course, is it a sin. 'Ten years ago,' wailed Mr. Prendergast, 'I was a clergyman of the Church of England. I had just been presented with a living in Worthing. It was an attractive church, not old, but very beautifully decorated, six candles on the Altar, Reservation in the Lady Chapel, and an excellent heating-apparatus which burnt coke in a little shed by the sacristy door. All very pleasant — *until my doubts began*.' 'Were they as bad as all that?' he was asked. 'They were insuperable,' was all that he could reply. Poor Mr. Prendergast! He couldn't have imagined he was the first ever to battle with such doubts. He couldn't have forgotten Thomas — 'Doubting Thomas', as he has come to be known down the years. I like to think of him as 'the man who became certain, by doubting'. When I made my visit to the proud city of Florence, my first request was to see Verrochio's sculpture, 'The Incredulity of St. Thomas'. Somehow, it brought him nearer to me than many another haloed saint in a stained-glass window.

It was unfortunate that Thomas was not with the disciples after the Crucifixion and Resurrection, when Jesus appeared among them; but on second thoughts, how fortunate for us. Where he was at the time, nobody knows; but his reaction was one that completely explodes the idea some have, that the early disciples, poor things, were simple, unlettered, credulous souls, ready at first sight to believe anything. *Oh, no!* One has only to look at Thomas, when he returned, and his friends met him with the news that they had seen Jesus. The New Testament says simply: 'Thomas was not with them when Jesus came.' Others could believe what they liked; he had no choice but to doubt. 'Except I shall see in His hands the print of the nails,' said he, 'and put my finger into the print of the nails, and thrust my hand into His side, I will not believe.' After eight days, when they were together, He appeared among them again — and this time, Thomas was with them. Not for a moment did He scold Thomas for his doubts; rather He met him patiently at the point of them: 'Reach hither thy finger', said He, 'and behold My hands; and reach hither thy hand, and thrust it into My side; and be not faithless, but believing. And Thomas answered, with the consent of all His faculties: *"My Lord and my God !"* '

The only way you and I can avoid doubt is to avoid life. Otherwise there is always this faith-doubt tension. Only those who contrive to skip thought and deep involvement can have it otherwise. 'Thomas,' says Dr. William Barclay, 'has been called "the twentieth-century saint". ' Whether one can justly claim that it is harder to believe the Christian Faith today, than at any other time, no one who thinks, can blame Thomas for wanting to be sure. Thomas's temperament seems to have been all prose — not poetry. He says, in effect: 'My dear fellows, don't try to put that over me. Your wishful-thinking has run away with you. I'm one, as you know, to keep my feet on the ground. This that you pretend is the last thing I'll believe.'

To me, at one time, it seemed strange that Thomas was even amongst the first bunch of disciples. It was only in the events recorded in John's Gospel that he emerged from the shadows — and unforgettably, in this greatest shadow of all. But then I did not early understand the necessity of doubt. Now I owe a debt to Thomas. And though none of us kin to him in temperament will ever experience such an emotional test as the crucifixion and burial of our closest friend, we know that emotional experiences bear greatly on doubts. All this worsened for Thomas because of his absence when his friends made their discovery — no one knows where he was, but I think he couldn't bear to be with them. He just wanted to go over it all alone.

There are some things that I am ready to accept on the excited word of others — the majesty of Mount Everest, the age of the *sequoia* under the Californian sky for two thousand years and more — but not the essentials of the Faith, above all, the Resurrection. On the living presence of Jesus today so much hangs. Thomas is not only the patron-saint of the perplexed, he is the patron-saint of the sincere seeker after reality. Dostoevsky has not been the only one to admit: 'My hosanna has passed through the great purgatory of doubt.' The important thing is that it has *passed through*. 'If ever I had any doubts about the fundamental realities of religion', said Alfred Noyes, 'they could always be dispelled by one memory — the light on my father's face as he came back from early Communion.' Says Dr. J. B. Phillips of our day: 'I was not born with my collar turned the wrong way round. In fact, I spent several years disbelieving in any kind of God at all! It took me a lot of hard thinking as well as some experience of life before I found the real God. So I am able to be patient with those who have not yet found their way to a faith which makes sense.'

This is 'honest doubt' — always ready to be led through to assurance, as patiently as Jesus dealt with poor Thomas. This is the experience of several others whom I greatly admire. William Temple was so tormented by doubts at one time, that he waited for years — whilst in heart-searching correspondence with the then Archbishop of Canterbury — before he felt he could proceed to ordination. That admission surprised me, for he seemed always to walk with such a sure tread, to become youthful Archbishop himself, leading in great conferences, speaking through the press, and writing learned and helpful Christian books. A number of them are the most helpful I possess.

And alongside them are those of another great spirit, to whom I owe much — Dr. Donald Baillie, brother of Dr. John Baillie. It was a great loss to his students — as to countless others of us — when he too, died prematurely, as did William Temple. John Baillie later told us that his scholarly, gracious, and so human brother, so robust, so sensitive, was 'haunted at one time by doubt'.

It becomes, I find, a source of strength to find our Lord meeting these, one by one — as He did Thomas — at the point of doubt. It might be to question the Genesis poetical account of Creation, in this scientific day; to query the account of a particular miracle; to accept the persuasive promise of the triumph of the Kingdom of God.

At the heart of steady Faith stands the Risen Christ —
whatever subsequent questioning might occur — and sure of
Him, one can go ahead. This reality is one's 'shaft of sunlight'.
'Whatever it is you are not sure of,' says Dr. Donald Baillie,
'at least you can go ahead. And if you do, persistently, faithfully, you will gradually come to be sure of something else,
too. You will come to feel that *the Voice calling you to these
things is not simply your own voice. It is not just the beating of
your own heart. It is the beating of the Heart of the Universe.*'

31

Landing in the Largest City

Since my heart had been troubling me for some time, it seemed
best, before the need arose to set out on a long trip, to try
myself out on a short one. I agreed to travel for the first time
with three friends, and on the understanding that at every
point, our luggage would be handled.

So it happened, that one calm night — travelling under the
steady stars — we came to the world's largest city, Tokyo. A
goodly representation of its millions seemed to be there to meet
us — a sea of black neat bristly heads, spreading out within the
air-port, where, obvious strangers by every reckoning, we were
obliged to present our documents.

Once outside, it was speeding traffic, and neon lights in many
colours everywhere, that held our interest — the radio and
television tower rising into the night sky, forty feet higher than
the famous Eiffel Tower of Paris. Its dominance we had no
way of checking for height ourselves: as next day we had no
way of confirming the figures we were given as representing the
eight thousand, four hundred and eighty-eight bridges the
city boasted. In the same way, we were obliged to accept —
beyond what our eyes could tell us — that the population ate
on an average daily six million pounds of rice, three and a

half million pounds of fish, and bought six million train-tickets. All very impressive! But it was not till these statistics took on faces, that we felt that the city did more for us, than hammer on our brains. It is always that way; and more than ever in Tokyo, where the street-numbers seemed to offer no kind of sequence. I can think of no more puzzling city in which to find one's way about.

Our age has been called 'the age of the shrug' — and lacking more than half-a-dozen words of Japanese in our little party — one could readily visualise a situation where that would be inevitable. We heard little of our own language — and saw little of it, save on a few marketable goods. I was amused to light upon a number of bright cans, each bearing quaint English: 'Safara-San Oysters, Packed in Japan with diligence and responsibility'. I liked its joint claim; responsibility, I knew, meant the 'ability to respond' — and I hoped I would find it, not only amidst oysters-packers, but amongst ordinary people. For a long time, the most-used word I had to offer, for my part, pushing amid street-throngs, was 'sumimasen' — Very sorry!

Students clustered around one continually in temple gardens; and night by night, came into the lounge of any hotel where we stayed, in twos and threes, courteously asking our aid with the little English they knew. Up a narrow lane that led to the Silver Pavilion in Kyoto, we found later, a hand-painted notice that a boy had fastened on the front of his house:

WELCOME

Let me guid you to be on intimate term with your country. You need not pay me because I wish to get only a friendship. And I am not a good speaker of English. I am a student of the Kyoto University. I am studying English conversation. If you need me and have lost yourself please open the door and say Hello!

Whenever we elected to take a taxi to any distant shrine, or art-centre, it was essential to have written down in Japanese our lodging address, the address to which we meant to be driven, and as clearly, the address to which we hoped to be returned.

Riding through the countryside by train — and one can travel out of Tokyo, in *the fastest in the world*, which we did — it was not possible to read each red character that a building bore. It was impossible — lacking the language — to know whether any building we passed, housed a boys' school, a hospital, or a shirt-factory.

*   *   *

Our earliest train-trip brought us two hours later, to Nikko — to a wonderful celebration at the Toshohu Shrine. We made the journey a day early, because sixty thousand persons, we were told, would line the way for the colourful procession, on the day set for the celebration.

This allowed us to approach by way of a great avenue of handsome cedar trees of which I had read — twenty thousand of them, dignified under the sky. The story told of them centred on the early building of the Shrine, when leaders of the people from near and far, brought gifts of gold, silver and pearl, and other rareties. But there was one poor land-owner who had nothing of the accepted kind to bring — and he brought instead bundles of little seedlings his men had up-rooted. Despite the scorn of many, they were eventually planted *en route* to the Shrine; and now, after years, they remained in honour, the only 'living gift' of that time!

The Shrine was early named in honour of the Generalissimo. We found the hilltop studded with sacred buildings, set as so many jewels, beautiful in red laquer, gold, and priceless gems.

One sight that took us by surprise was the original of 'The three little monkeys', met first in childhood. (Copied, painted and modelled, they had gone out from here to the ends of the earth.) Beginning from the left, outside the sacred stable, the first held its hands over its ears, the next held its hands over its mouth, the third over its eyes. Together, by their actions, they have persisted through the centuries, in saying :'*Hear* no evil, *speak* no evil, *see* no evil!' As the simple poem says:

They sit in their wisdom, the Three
The little deaf monkey,
The little dumb monkey,
And the monkey who will not see.

But it was a wonder — it suddenly there dawned upon me — that parents hadn't long ago seen what a negative thing it was. There was all the difference between 'Don't!' and 'Do!'

*   *   *

Back in Tokyo, I sought out another animal-likeness — and one that pleased me much more. It stood in front of the Shibuya Railway-station, one of the busiest terminals, where are set seats, and a tree or two. It was the likeness of a friendly-looking dog, that one couldn't help but find attractive, sitting as if waiting for a romp. His name, I learned, without much effort, was Hachiko.

Hachiko had been the fond companion of his master, whom he had seen off every morning at the station, and welcomed back every evening. Suddenly — on May 21st, 1924, whilst away from home, his master had died. Faithful Hachiko had, of course, no means of knowing this sad fact. Expecting him to return, as usual, each evening he continued to trot to the station. And he kept up this for *eleven years*!

People were moved by this beautiful faithfulness — when the Dog Preservation Society made it known — and they began to send in money-gifts to put up a figure of him during the last year of his life. Very strikingly, they didn't wait until Hachiko died; and they were supported in this gesture, beyond their own shores, by a number of American admirers. That was in 1934. But when conditions became difficult for the Japanese people during World War II, and many metal objects in the city were melted down, the figure had to go. Many were sad at that.

But they kept alive in their hearts the memory of Hachiko; and as soon as it became possible — two years after the war ended — they set about gathering funds to make a new statue. And this they set up in August, 1948 — people far away, again helping. And fittingly — as I discovered — the little place where the tribute of such faithfulness now stands, is called 'Hachiko Plaz'.

*   *   *

Some days later — in Hiroshima, of all places — I found faithfulness of another kind. When first I had considered going there, I wondered if I had courage enough to gaze upon the scene of that unprecedented holocaust, a shame on the human race. The *New Statesman* — claiming no avowedly Christian standing — had headed its leader on the Friday after that sombre happening: 'Who shall control omnipotence?' The moral responsibility implied seemed too much to face. So I felt. But I am thankful that I made time to go to renewed Hiroshima, where war, Judas-like, had kissed the city with Atom's breath, committing young and old alike, to black contorted death. That grim day in August 1945, cast away 76,341 men, women and children and named the city 'The Atomic Desert'. 'A list of names of additional persons dying from the lingering effects of the blast is added annually at the memorial services held on August 6th.' A number of shattered buildings remain — an impressive filigree against the sky, in the case of one tall one — and a symbol of suffering is to be seen, along with an arch bearing an un-dying flame, and a children's memorial for those who among others, loving life, that moment became statistics.

It was moving to read the report of the Japanese newspaper-man — correspondent of *The New York Times* — the *first* to pass on the news to the horror-stricken world. He saw his responsibility in that grim experience as two-fold in human terms — to report the happening, and to find one beloved person, his own mother.

In the final issue that is how it is — the individual always steps out of the crowd in one's concern. This, in a marked degree, the people of Hiroshima seem to have achieved — having called their city, once 'The Atomic Desert', now 'The City of Peace'. Seemingly, revenge has no place there; instead, there is readiness and every facility for International Peace Conferences to be held. And many hospitals and homes exist to minister to those who still suffer — I talked with two, husband and wife, who fortunately for me, had a little English. One centre of healing compassion for aged people interested me specially — a nursing-home with the striking name '*Seireien*' — 'Garden of clear ringing bells'. Within a country where are few Christians per population, this was built by the Churches, with the help of American friends who heard of the venture. So miracles go on to this hour, even in unlikely places.

I couldn't help but think it ironical that the Atom-bomb was dropped in August — in what is O-Bon, 'The Season of the Dead'. At that time, one by one, members of a family who chance to be afar, make an effort to come back to their birth-place, or to their parents, to burn incense and pay tribute to their honoured dead at the small family altar, or at the local shrine or temple. So it happened that many were away from Hiroshima when Death descended; and as many were visiting who normally wouldn't have been there. Happily, now, her-bage, grass, trees and flowers appear again — to discover as much was as 'a shaft of sunlight' on my spirit — I had been given to understand at the time of the incineration that nothing could ever be expected to bloom again.

On the morning of the 6th, a young girl, Junko Itose — a pupil of the Methodist Mission School — set off to the station to meet a friend. She never did meet her — for she vanished, as did the station. But the schoolgirl, Junko somehow survived, through the stunning, baffling chaos, choking sensations and hospital — and an innocent girl emerged later to marry in time a young British soldier, and to move to a neat English home on the fringes of Cheltenham. As thousands listened a while ago on B.B.C. T.V. she told her story in the new language she had learned, and many marvelled that out of her confused mem-ories, Junko Itose could bring forth such forgiveness 'seventy-times-seven'. But this is a world in which miracles do happen!

32

'Pearls For A Pearl'

One of the plans I made when I knew that I was going to Japan, ushered in a day of utter delight. For some time I had known Mikimoto's story. And by car and boat it now seemed that I could visit his island home.

Beginning as a small boy, he earned his modest living from selling noodles in the streets. But all the while, he cherished a dream — one day he would own a pearl so beautiful that it would be worth all that he called his own to possess it.

Whilst still young, he was invited to accompany another on a first visit to Tokyo. It was a great excitement. His chief interest there was in watching the pearl-merchants. 'What do you want?' asked one. 'Just to look,' was the lad's reply. For a very long time after that unforgettable experience he had no money to do more.

A grain of sand, or some other irritant, he knew, had to lodge inside the oyster shell before a pearl could be created. To relieve the irritation, the mollusc would then produce a secretion. As it went on doing this, it reached a certain thickness, and solidified layer by layer, to become a superb nacre, an almost spherical pearl. But it took a long, long time to achieve this, in the way that Nature had always worked. And thousands and thousands of shells never knew any such irritant — any such nacre.

Holding his youthful dream through the years, it occurred to the young seeker to insert an irritant of his own choosing — thus giving more shells a chance of producing a pearl. The shells, of course, had to be handled with great care, lest the living oyster should be damaged, or worse, killed altogether.

Mikimoto had first to get hold of a few thousand shells. Then he opened each as carefully as he could, and inserted his chosen irritant. Then choosing a suitable stretch of the sea-coast, he racked his shells together, and put them back into their native element.

There was a good deal of chance about his undertaking, he knew, since it had never been done before. Was it possible to help Nature in the way he had assumed it was? Some years had to pass. Meanwhile he had to continue with the sale of noodles.

At last the time came to test his plan. But when the shells were prized open one by one, there was not a single pearl within any one of them.

What had gone wrong? Was the irritant too large, too coarse, or of the wrong kind? Mikimoto could only guess at the answer he sought, and try again. This meant another out-lay for shells, and another long wait. When the news got out, the people of Toba said: 'Mikimoto is *baka* — stupid,' using that strongest word they knew for such a state. But the pearl-seeker took no notice — though his debts mounted, and his patience was long tested. He was in no mood to give up his dream. By this time, he was a married man with a growing family. But Ume, his little wife, gave him every support. She was ready to take charge of the noodles, as the modest source of their income. When the time came to lift the shells, she spent hour after hour with him wet through, opening the shells. But again, the dream had been at the mercy of enemy fish, boisterous winds, and the poisonous red tide. To give up, at that point, would have been to fail utterly. The only thing was to try again. And this they did — with the long wait, and care of another lot of shells meanwhile. By this time, it had become plain to Mikimoto that the tiny piece of irritant had been inserted improperly — instead of placing it between the flesh and the shell, he should have placed it in the flesh of the mollusc itself. So the search continued.

After much more work, a day came never to be forgotten — and what a day it was! Mikimoto could hardly believe his eyes — before him was his perfect pearl! And soon this was followed by others. 'I will not pretend that I have not helped Nature,' he said frankly to Ume, and then to those concerned in the outside world. 'But each pearl, nevertheless, is of Nature's own patient making.'

Soon his 'cultured pearls' were appearing in the market. But there were men there who strenuously contested his right to sell them. The eventual outcome was a case before the Court, in Paris. But Mikimoto won his case — experts supporting him — and was able to satisfy the authorities that his pearls were completely genuine.

Soon, Mikimoto and Ume and his family needed the help of others in their growing enterprise. They lived modestly, and employed diving-girls to help. All who served the development of his pearls were well paid for their work, and provided for — the first work-girls in the land to be granted an eight-hour day.

But it did not take long before shabby copyists were offering *their* pearls in the market — without the care that Mikimoto took to see that each was perfect in shape and coloration. This grieved Mikimoto, and he bought up seven hundred and fifty thousand of their poor-grade pearls. Then giving public notice of what he meant to do, he shovelled them on to a bonfire in the crowded streets of Kobe. Passers-by were astonished; but nobody any more questioned Mikimoto's standard — and the world's newspapers soon called the story 'Pearls for a Pearl!'

(I was too late to meet the old pearl-seeker myself — he had died in 1954, aged ninety-four — but a bronze likeness of him stood under the wide sky, as I stepped ashore on his little island. And later — after I had seen shells raised from the sea, one was placed in my hand, and opened there to reveal a pearl!)

And every time now that I read the New Testament account of the Pearl of Great Price, I recall that miracle happening: 'The Kingdom of God,' the New Testament says plainly, 'is like unto a man that is a merchant seeking goodly pearls; and having found *one of great price*, he went and sold all that he had and bought it' (Matthew 13: 45–46).

He was a buyer of pearls, scholars now help me to realise, who for a dream like Mikimoto's, continually kept his eye open for pearls of worth wherever he went. One day, we are led to know, he met a man who could say: 'I have one pearl that I believe will interest you — the most lustrous and perfectly formed that you've ever seen.' No time was lost in inspecting it. Eagerly, he learned the price. 'Hold it for me,' was all that the eager seeker could say. 'I'll have to sell all my small pearls — but I'll find the price of it somehow.'

And with quickened step, and eyes bright, off home he went to gather up what pearls he already owned. He was not going to lose now what he so longed for; and soon, he was back to conclude the deal with the merchant.

It is a story to emphasise unforgettably now, the cost of the best. The seeker — like Mikimoto — was prepared for any cost, that he might acquire the one perfect pearl. *It was Pearls for a Pearl!* When I shared this 'shaft of sunlight' with my friend, Dr. D. T. Niles, he immediately underlined to me, its teaching: 'The Great Pearl, the Kingdom of God, *is only bought by selling small pearls*. Where no pearl has been sold' said he, 'then obedience to the demands of the Kingdom has not begun.' It costs — in this deep-down, continuing choice! But the 'true seeker' recognises it for what it is, a wonderful bargain!

31

Wonder into Worship

The last few minutes whilst the plane-engines were revving-up to sound like a million bee-hives, used to terrify me — but not now. Though I confess to a few qualms at the other end, when we touched-down in Hong Kong — *en route* to Japan — on what looked like a mere cricket-pitch, cast into the sea, surrounded by sentinel hills. At night, when the city and hills were glow-wormed with coloured lights, that strip seemed more forbidding than ever — but somehow, planes managed to come and go. And we got up.

After our rewarding stay in Japan, the engines revved up once more — to lift us with a thousand new experiences in our lives, and a score of purchased gifts, and pieces of hand-work in our luggage — on to Taiwan, '*Ilha Formosa*', beautiful island, as the Portuguese discoverers rejoiced to call it.

When Abel Jansen Tasman — discoverer of my little land, first glimpsed it — it was to this green, irregular terrain that his thoughts flew, and finding what he took to be a comparison ready made, wrote of New Zealand as 'a land uplifted high, with a high mountain range, not lower than the island of Formosa'.

But there — for me, at any rate, the comparison must end — since 'the beautiful island', Taiwan, as it is now called, is shaped like a lozenge, some two hundred and eighty miles from end to end, and ninety miles across at its widest. And it has a population of nearly eleven million. Nowhere, in any of New Zealand's cities — unless it is at the lunch-break, or at five o'clock when offices close, and people pour into the streets — have I seen such crowds as in Taipei. And, of course, we lack an Asian atmosphere — tri-shaws, fruit stalls on the kerbside, lightly-clad people in sweltering heat — and never before had I seen, even in Japan, such a fabulous building as the hotel in which we stayed, overlooking the city of Taipei. Built and decorated in Mandarin palace style — with bright red lacquered pillars at its front, and the glamour and luxury of gilded screens within, and a philosophical legend of comfort carved on each bed-end.

On every bit of vacant wall-space in the city was a large picture of Chang Kai Shek, and what we couldn't help but feel to be a rather plaintive dream about 'The recovery of the Mainland'. One was left wondering how it could be achieved. We had each read a good deal about Chang Kai Shek — but he was now an ageing leader.

*   *

The most memorable experience of our stay — not surprisingly — had nothing to do with politics. Journeying deep into the country by plane, and by train, and car, we arrived at Sun-Moon Lake. A delightful Asian name! There, we discovered, Chang Kai Shek had his country conference-centre. Though discreetly locked and shuttered, it turned out to be a modest adjunct to our hotel. One climbed winding mountain roads through towns and villages, and lush green areas of sugar-cane and tea, to find it set high on the brink of the lake-shore. 'There used to be two lakes here, side by side,' I learned, on enquiry. 'They were linked together since the beginning of time, at the head of this loveliest of valleys. One was round, so it was called "Sun Lake", the other crescent-shaped, so it was called "Moon Lake". Only a little ridge of hills divided them.' In recent times, when the need for a hydro-electric project arose, the outlets were dammed, and as the waters rose, the two lakes became one. With sweet reasonableness, characteristic of the people, they solved the matter simply by calling the result 'Sun-Moon Lake'.

Here and there, hilltops that had not been submerged, made gem-like islands. On one such — a little out from our balcony that hung on the edge of the lake-cliff — was supported a little temple. Here — the clock round — prayers were offered for the realisation of the dream: 'Back to the Mainland?' When the sounds of day were hushed, though they were few and modest, we could hear the voice of the priest in beautiful solitude chanting the prayers. There was something very wistful about it. We couldn't help wondering how different things would be by his life's end, and whether others would go on praying that prayer.

Our most wonderful experience happened next morning — wonderful, in the truest sense, because it was full of wonder. Someone told us not to miss the sunrise; and we talked it over together and agreed, all four of us, in those two rooms on the cliff-edge overlooking the Lake, to rise in time and move out on to the balcony. It was still dark when, in our wraps, we appeared. Soon, the slightest hint of light was showing.

The first soft shafts of light came down from between the mountains onto the silver waters of the lake. There was no least sound to be heard anywhere — it was like the dawn of Creation. The mountains rose in abrupt Chinese shapes, squared across the top, as we had seen them reproduced on lacquered chests, and on screens. At first, they stood sentinel, silhouetted against the sky, just a little deeper colour than the lake.

As we stood, awaiting what would happen by the dictates of the World's Great Artist, a tiny boat — poled by one man, wearing a flattish V-shaped hat — started out across the shimmering silver waters, from the left hand corner of our view. Just beyond the dark fringe of great trees below us he appeared — crossing at an angle, and leaving a strip pattern behind him on the placid lake.

No one spoke. All the time he made his way, filling in the picture; all the time further shafts of light were coming from between the mountains, until the sun was fully risen.

How long we stood there — like worshippers in the dawn I can't tell; nor have I any assurance that I have re-told this wonder worthily. We four friends have spoken of that moment, since — and each of us felt the same about it.

I cannot send another to Taiwan — complete with tourist's tickets and camera-lenses — to see a sunrise. He might retort that he could do that at home, if he bothered to set the alarm. We can't agree — there was something specially *wonderful* about this! Alfred Noyes has spoken well: 'Only fools have said that knowledge drives *out wonder* from the world.' If anyone objects that Noyes was a poet, then I am ready with the words of a down-to-earth modern, credited with the greatest mind active in our day, Albert Einstein. Says he: 'The most beautiful, the most profound emotion we can experience is the sensation of the mystical. It is the power of all true Science. He to whom this emotion is a stranger, *who can no longer wonder* and stand rapt in awe, is as good as dead ... This knowledge, this feeling is at the centre of all true religiousness.'

He would have understood our silence — as would Professor Tyndall (to name but two, along with Noyes, the poet). Professor Tyndall never forgot his *wonder-ful* experience of ascending the White Alp. It was evening when he reached the top, and there by himself, opened his note-book to jot down some scientific observation. But as he stood, he beheld the glory of the Alps — white peaks smitten by the sword-beams of the setting sun, until they flamed on a sea of glory, mingled with fire. It was so magnificent, so divine, that he confessed, 'I put my note-book in my pocket. I returned my pencil to its sheath. *I felt the hour of worship had struck!*'

30

'The Beauty of Bread'

Back home!

I cross the city two or three times a year to share a meal with a friend, a retired nurse, living alone at the top of a neat garden. She serves a delicious meal always — but this week something was added. 'I've a surprise for you,' said she, with face alight, 'something I've never made before.'

I was curious. And when the platter came, it held months of sunlight, weeks of rain, good earth, and spacious sky — and soon I was eating those good nourishing primal gifts. For it was a golden-crusted home-made loaf that she set before me. And soon I was being told how she had made it — bread-making plainly an occupation conducive to sharing at every level — the kneading and shaping of the responsive dough, the patient baking, and the matchless delight awaiting the senses when the oven was opened.

Giving my attention to pleasurable reflection later, on returning home, I set down as title of a poem: 'The Beauty of Bread.'

The first bread I tasted came from my mother's
      oven,
gold-crusted, sweetest of the gifts of
      earth
made from the best flour, from the best
      grain
grown in the sun-blessed countryside that gave
      me birth.

Working till the shadows lengthened to
      night,
in the mill by the stream I came to love as
      my own,
the miller, white in sacramental dust,
      fulfilled
the hope with which the seed had been
      sown.

Till this present breath, I have thought much
      of bread —
of soil tilled, seed sown, and tended
      with care,
rain and sun each bringing a gift without
      cost —
that the hungry of earth might learn how
      to share.

[R.F.S.]

One thing is certain — always has been — solitary bread is not the same as that shared with another. Alone, it nourishes but the body; our Lord knew that, and taught us to pray: 'Give *us* this day *our* daily bread.' And no prayer rises today more consistently from earth to heaven, in the languages we share — 'Our Father . . . *our* daily bread.' Many who offer it, like our Lord Himself — are on the bread-line. But there is a solidarity about that prayer: 'Our Father', in heaven, implies 'our brother, on earth'.

Never a month passes but somewhere, harvesting is in full swing, by the sweat of the brow, New Zealand, and Chile lead off with their in-gathering in Janauary. Parts of India and Upper Egypt follow in February and March. The remainder of India's harvest is gathered in April. Syria, Asia Minor, and Persia follow on in May. June brings in the harvest of Italy, Spain, Turkey, and Southern France. Harvest extends over three months in the United States. South Russia gathers in her harvest in July — as do Bulgaria, Rumania, Hungary and Germany. Central Russia, Poland, Canada, and England gather in August and September. September sees harvesting in Northern Russia, too. October shifts the scene to Sweden and Norway. November brings the harvesters to South Africa into the fields, and the year is rounded off with the harvesting of Australia, Argentina, and Abyssinia. So every month, somewhere in the world, men and women are helping to answer the prayer for bread. This is God's way: He does not put bread into our hands without effort.

Some of the sturdiest people of the earth eat only dark bread. In the Middle Ages, it was called 'maslin bread' — maslin being the same as 'miscelin', or 'mixed', made of rye and wheat, with an occasional addition of barley and oats. White bread — miscalled 'chalk, alum and plaster' by some — has only won favour in relatively recent times. Chaucer's 'poor widow' ate from a brown loaf, and in the time of Richard-the-Lion-heart, rye for bread was grown almost as widely as wheat. Cromwell's soldiers all ate bread made of three-parts rye.

But bread — brown or white — has been continually prayed for, and continually toiled for. Nothing in our modern age of tractors, fertilisers, and agricultural skills has changed this. We are still dependent on God for sun, rain and growth; we are still inter-dependent with our fellows who till, harvest, make flour, bake and share. This being so, we cannot regard bread lightly.

It is a grief that whilst two out of three the world round go hungry to bed, and wake hungry to face the new day, a great number over-eat. My editorial friend, Frances Russell, offers much more than a chuckle in her '*Grace for the comfortably off*':

God bless this food
Superfluous,
And may it put
No weight on us. Amen.

Donald Faris is eager that we shall not escape awareness of the situation. 'Visualise', says he, 'a line from your front door, made up of the hungry of the world. The line goes on and out of sight, over continent and ocean, around the whole world — 25,000 miles — and returns to your door — not once, twice or five times, but *twenty-five*! And there is no one in that line, but is a member of hungering, suffering humanity!'

Somehow, I must brace my imagination to reckon with that line reaching out from my door — when I pray: '*Our* Father . . . *our* daily bread.' I must keep it in the forefront of my mind, when I am tempted to be wasteful in any way.

It is true, one cannot live by bread alone; but without bread, one cannot even live to pray for it. In this world, we are all 'guests of God' — and in a very involved sense, all 'servants of one another'. *Bread matters so much — because in our Father's world, people matter so much!*

To reduce one's weekly provision-bill, somehow, is a laudable response to the grim estimate of the number who died last week from hunger — if one sends on the money to Christian Aid. But it is not enough, for there is as well, the vastly greater number caught up in what Barbara Ward, one of our finest Christian economists, calls 'creeping famine.' 'There are', she told her listeners lately over the B.B.C., 'something like 320 million children who are under-nourished to the pitch that they probably will never grow to their full human potential. They are not getting protein when they need it, in infancy, so that their brains can grow. It is creeping death. Unless we can counter that with a *protein strategy*, with the acceptance that the planet needs a food plan, then I think we are already in the middle of death, death and more death.'

Behind this food strategy lies the need for thousands of wells, and for the enrichment of impoverished soil, and for the best producing grains. This is the only way that people can be helped to help themselves. Fortunate countries are already supplying beasts to build up better herds, and skilled men and women to show how this can be done. The need seems tremendous; but I know little groups of concerned people in a number of communities, and congregations of Christians who have set themselves to fast one day weekly to make a regular gift toward wells. Water is so desperately needed — for the watering of growing crops, and the drinking needs of beasts and people. A hundred dollars can sink a well in India, to name but one needy country — a plan well within the reach of most clubs and congregations in multiples of a hundred persons in this well-fed land.

One need never apologise for talking about bread in a hungry world.

35

As Whole Persons

More than once I have been a patient in hospital; and for many long months, in my twenties, was patient at home — coming to terms with a scarred heart, that I have lived with ever since. So I know a little of what the world looks like to one on the horizontal.

Mercifully, medical care has shown enormous improvement, even in my lifetime, not to mention the unfolding centuries. Lately, I plucked from a history-book the almost callous report of poor King Charles II. 'A pint of blood', it said, 'was extracted from the royal right arm, and a half-pint from the royal left shoulder, followed by an emetic. The royal head was then shaved, and a blister raised; then a sneezing-powder was given; and a plaster of pitch put on the patient's feet. Finally, forty drops of extract of human scull was given, after which,' the account finishes, 'his Majesty gave up the ghost.' Imagine it! The shock of such treatment, without anaesthesia, was surely enough to bring any patient to death, without reckoning on his particular illness. If this was the best available for a royal patient, then let us pity the commoner.

It is not impossible to estimate how much we rightly owe to those who have devoted their energies and skills to medical service up through the centuries; Christian compassion has supported it all the way. The first asylum for the blind was founded by a Christian monk, Thalasius; the first free dispensary was opened by Apollonius, a Christian merchant; the first hospital of which there is any record, was established by a Christian lady, Fabiola. The Christian Church has proved itself — in any missionary land — more ready than the government of the time, to begin to alleviate human suffering, and to train others to carry on.

We have come a long way — in early times there was much callousness and quackery. Even for a mild fever, the prescription was 'a live fresh-water fish tied to the feet for twelve hours, then buried quietly'. (One supposes this meant the fish, and not the patient, though that is not clear.)

After John Masefield, Poet Laureate in our day, was discharged from hospital, he wrote a tribute to the nurses who had tended him, beginning: 'Let me honour those who tend the patients when the doctor goes.'

Tributes are constantly paid to nurses, in one way and another. The profession needs the best today — as much, if not more, than when Florence Nightingale first clothed it with dignity and honour. Today, nurses are encouraged to think of their patients as *whole persons* — not just bodies.

(A few fall below this high standard; but for most nursing is a vocation.)

*   *   *

The same is as true of Hospital Chaplains. Their services have never been so well-honoured. As patient himself — and later Chaplain — no one I know is more aware of the nature of this 'wholeness' than my friend Archie Kirkwood.

At University, he won his blues for cross-country running; and two years in succession — still a record — he won the Port Chalmers to Dunedin road-race.

With such a background, a sudden illness in 1968 — resulting in paralysis — posed unguessed handicaps. A young Presbyterian minister, immersed in Parish interests, he was in his pulpit in Invercargill on the morning of that Sunday never-to-be-forgotten, and before the afternoon closed, he was in the Intensive-Care Unit in hospital. 'Think of it,' he said to me, lately, 'I had to be fed; and I had to be turned every two hours; I could not use hands or feet.'

But set to a stiffer race than he had then known — he has won through, nothing wasted — as Reverend A. McG. Kirkwood, 'Wheel-chair Chaplain', at Green Lane and at National Women's Hospitals, in our city. Moving from bed to bed in his electric wheel-chair, he explains 'I have a little understanding of how patients feel ... And one practical advantage is that physically, I am on their level. Patients sometimes are over-awed by people who stand over them.'

Archie sees his role of Hospital Chaplain as 'bringing in the help of Christ to others, in a positive way'. He is a listening-post, a counsellor, a constant friend available. His own on-going struggle gives him an advantage — he does not do this work as a man of 'words only'. His ready smile and cheerful approach spell much more than a genial disposition. When he regards hospitals as 'centres of hope', he means what he says. His wife — a trained nurse — drives him to and from hospital daily — otherwise, his present speed is much limited.

But one is not long in the Chaplain's company at home, or on the job, without hearing from him a tribute of thankfulness — to the sustaining power of Christ, to his wife and teenage sons, and to the Hospital staff and praying Church-group about him from the beginning. His very first doctor, he discovered in his need, was an Egyptian — of the Coptic Church. 'He said to my wife,' the Chaplain now recalls, 'when I was critically ill, "Pray"! To me he repeated, "Prayer and Faith, Courage . . ." One evening later when I felt moved to thanks, his reply was, "Don't thank me, thank God! This is God's work, isn't it?" ' Months passed slowly. ' "I want you," ' said the Doctor, "to get a job, and preach, and tell what God has done for you — and kick your legs to show." ' This was hope, if anything could be. Hospitals are immersed in continual crises. And now that the Chaplain ministers to staff, relations and friends involved, as well as to the patients, he knows well what prayer and hope mean — and how much the backing of a congregation of caring people counts. Apart from the hurts physical, and nervous, there are often personal fears, domestic problems, and religious queries to help sort out. A sick person must be ministered to as a *whole* person. Bed to bed visitation, regular worship services, and rounds with the requested elements of the Communion, bear this in mind. And there are lectures to nurses in training to fit in — on such all-important issues as 'The Spiritual needs of patients': 'Pain and Suffering'; 'Dying' — each in the on-going pattern of personal respect for the patient, who often feels insecure in a strange bed, in a strange place, with strange people. In an 'island of pain', intense loneliness may be added to all else; the very 'sights, sounds, medicinal smells and techniques' add to this. 'To the patient,' concludes my friend the Chaplain, understandably, 'illness is a crisis — short, sharp, or long drawn-out . . . Our joint approach is to a whole person.'

*   *   *

My contribution to this ministry, as a writer, has lately been a paperback: *When my Visitors go*. Its Preface begins:

This little book can give no glib answers to the problem of suffering. Volumes have already been written on what men have puzzled out.

But it can be practical, and offer a handful of Prayers, Readings, Meditations and Affirmations. One thing it can say plainly — on the authority of Jesus — suffering is not to be reckoned punishment for sin. [And this first came to me as 'a shaft of sunlight.'] He talked of the men on whom the Tower of Siloam fell: 'Think you that they were sinners above all men who dwelt in Jerusalem? I tell you, Nay!' (Luke 13: 4-5.)

Suffering, like the rain, falls on the just and the unjust — religion does not undertake to keep us safe ... God has fashioned us to live on a family-pattern. (If one lets his drains run foul, others about him will suffer; if a father drowns his wits in drink, his family can hardly avoid suffering. A slippery front step can bring down one's best friend — and carelessness of other kinds affects others. One can unwittingly break health-laws; and in a world of material things, unaccountable accidents occur.)

Though it is impossible here to unravel the age-old problem, it would be a pity to withhold the help that can be given. This is centred on the certainty that God cares, and blesses every effort to heal. Suffering may be painful, and puzzling — but it need not be utterly wasted; some flowers of character flourish this way.

[R.F.S.]

36

'*How Old Is Old?*'

The answer forthcoming when one asked this question, must have been very different in an earlier century — the fourteenth, fifteenth, sixteenth, seventeenth, eighteenth, nineteenth. Miracle-drugs in our day are continually pushing back the frontier of old-age, though it has still to be met. Plato, in his day, argued that the disciples of Hippocrates were guilty of a serious mischief, if by their healing skills they were able to stretch out life for any beyond their span of usefulness. Petrarch presented the same argument. And I have heard it even in our day. Though when it comes to considering the preciousness of our own lives, most of us would be unwilling to settle for the Psalmist's 'three score years and ten.'

Never before have I given much thought to the age of our animals and pets. The life of a horse, I am told, is twenty-seven years; that of a goat, fifteen; that of a sheep, twelve; of a rabbit, five.

The oldest living creature with which I have had dealings was the famous tortoise, Tui Malila, at the Palace on Tonga. When I was guest of Queen Salote, I had the opportunity of making his acquaintance. Kneeling beside him on his patch of grass, I was photographed, as many visitors before me had been. I asked about his exact age; but nobody could tell me. It was history that he was brought to Tonga by Captain Cook, in his little wooden sailing-vessel in 1770 — but nobody had been able to learn how old he was at the time. For a long time, I was assured, Tui Malila had been treated like a prince — a portion of every Royal feast saved for him. Though for some time this custom had been discontinued, he still had a full-time member of the Palace staff devoted to his welfare. And when Queen Elizabeth and the Duke paid their brief visit to Tonga, Queen Salote, their royal hostess, led them out to be photographed with Tui Malila. No other living creature of such an age, can have been photographed with two reigning queens — though I can't think he properly valued his honour. Nor can I think he had any adequate idea of time.

Some time before this, I took a little child on her first visit to the local zoo. It was full of surprises for her. At every cage we came to, she wanted to put her fingers through the bars to stroke the creature there. I had to explain that we could not do this — it was dangerous. Then we came to the zoo's tortoise on a patch of green. 'Now, this fellow is different,' I was able to say. You can stroke him. He is friendly — and *very very old*!' And without uttering a word, she moved over to stroke him, and seemed satisfied to stay longer than I had planned. When we got home that night — not a word about

him having been said *en route* — my little companion
rushed into the house ahead of me, to exclaim: 'Gran, what
do you think we saw ? *A b-e-e-t-l-e twice as old as you !*'

Who can say what a year, twenty years, a hundred, means
to such a creature ? But then, we speak of Time so loosely ourselves, often. I think, in this connection, of the poetic beauty
of the Old Testament record of Jacob's love-affair — spread
over an abnormally long patience-testing time. 'Jacob,' it says,
'served seven years for Rachel: and they seemed unto him but
a few days, for the love that he had to her' (Genesis 29: 20).
At the other extreme — and no less true — Jane Oliver the
novelist reminds me, that 'a life-time can lie, it seems, between
two strokes of the clock'. And I know this in experience —
having in one glimpse of a wood awash with bluebells, happened on my first English spring; having knelt a moment in
the silence of the crypt of Canterbury Cathedral; having entered upon the rich delight of Mozart's music with the first
few bars of one of his sonatas.

One of our distinguished scholars — Berdyaev — arguing
that Time earns its significance in depth, not in duration —
says: 'Life in Time remains without meaning, if it does not
receive its meaning from Eternity.'

Is this the meaning of our Lord's brief life-time — but
thirty-three years ? Before that limited adventure was expen-
ded, His disciples found Him saying to them: 'It is expedient
for you that I go away.' And in all too short a time, He had
passed out of some men's sight, that in a new dimension, He
might be near all men's hearts. His life certainly got its meaning
from Eternity!

Thirty-three years is a very short time, in which to do all
that He did! Dr. W. Fitchett, in our day, sums it up strikingly:
'One name alone is stamped on the brow of the hurrying
centuries . . . Jesus Christ! Here is a peasant in the darkest age
of the world, in a subject province. He never wrote a sentence
which has been preserved; He died cast out by His own race.
and abandoned by His scanty handful of followers. And yet,
twenty centuries after He hung on the Cross, His birth is
accepted by believers and unbelievers alike, as the point whence
all the centuries must be counted . . . *He has lifted, with pierced
hands, empires off their hinges.*'

So the length of Time is not all. We have additionãl proof of this in the life of many a follower of the Young Man of Galilee; I think of one of the most widely-known in our generation — Dietrich Bonhoeffer. A young German minister of acute mind and utter devotion, he died a prisoner just before the end of World War II. He wrote a good deal; and much has since been written of him, by others. After he had preached his last sermon to fellow-prisoners at a tiny service, the Gestapo entered with the order: 'Prisoner Bonhoeffer, get ready to come with us.' He knew all too well what that meant; and on his way out, he said to a young Englishman, a fellow-worshipper: *'This is the end — for me the beginning of Life.'*

So Life reaches out beyond Time — though what has gone into our span here, brief at its longest, we verily believe matters in the Hereafter. And even here it counts. Twenty years after young Bonhoeffer's death, Christians all round the world held thanksgiving services. One speaker, Dr. W. A. Visser Hooft, General Secretary of the World Council of Churches, at a service in Berlin, declared that in spite of his brief span of years, 'Bonhoeffer had yet exercised a greater influence on the contemporary Christian Church than any other member of his generation.'

The simple truth is that we are not children of Time — our Faith reaches out into the kingdom of Eternal values. The Bible, we find, nowhere attempts to argue the continuance of Life beyond our time here — it assumes it, just as it assumes the existence of God. To be sure, in the Old Testament, the reality of the Hereafter was dimly held — but by our young Lord's day in New Testament times, it was strongly held. 'Because I live,' said He, 'you shall live also' (John 14: 19). And again: 'Fear not them that kill the body, but are not able to kill the soul' (Matthew 10: 28). It was very little to be told — but coming from Him, it was enough. Paul, in his day, added compellingly: 'What shall separate us from the love of Christ? Shall ... life, shall death? *Nay!*' (Romans 8: 35–37). In our day, Dr. William Temple — youthful Archbishop of Canterbury, who came, like Bonhoeffer, all too early to his death, said of Life beyond Time as we know it: 'There is nothing in the world of which I am so certain. I have no idea what it will be like — and I am glad that I have not. I do not want it as *mere continuance*, but I want it for my understanding of life here. "God is love" appears to me nonsense in view of this world He has made if there is no other.'

My own mother — dying at fifty-two — had no hint that she had reached her life-limit in Time. She was happily engaged in her home-making interests as one evening drew on — and in a few moments, she was gone. There was only time to bring in a neighbour, a dear Christian nurse. With her face strangely radiant, I was told, my mother uttered but one name, as if in recognition: 'Jesus Christ!' I cannot know the fullness of what that meant to her; but I can't think that it held any fear. All her life here she had nourished her spirit on the expectation of Life beyond Time. And in turn, Paul's words sustain my spirit: 'Eye hath not seen, nor ear heard, neither had entered into the heart of man, the things which God hath prepared for them that love Him' (1 Corinthians 2: 9). Further than that I cannot go.

Though it seems certain we shall be delivered from our bodily limitations — our physical bodies exchanged for spiritual bodies, though in some degree associated with the life we know here, even as the seed sown is associated with the beautiful flower which bursts from it (Verses 43, 44). Another thing as certain — on the assurance of Scripture — is that we shall be delivered from the limitations, and the pains of these bodies — and from the transient, the tempting, the anxious, the grievous. In the final book of the New Testament, are words that are very meaningful to me: (Revelation 22: 3), 'His servants shall serve Him.' It is impossible to think that no use will there be made of all the qualities of personality we have tried our best to develop here; of what use are they, unless they matter lastingly? 'Let not your heart be troubled,' are our young Lord's words; 'ye believe in God, believe also in Me' (John 14: 1). Beyond that I do not ask to go.

A breath brought me
into this inheritance, speaking the syllables of Time —
to golden 'shafts of sunlight',
slender grass stalks,
bees in velvet, murmuring,
paths made by other feet across friendly fields,

hills crowned with challenge,
and hints only of the dark spaces
between my stars.

All purpose once
was in an hour, all summer in a flower —
weed-patterns in Mill-waters,
quick minnows playing
their hide-and-seek, mocking time and care,
soil's primal delight
sending life's plough down the furrow,
merging work and hope, white gulls
following after.

Till birth brought me,
how could I know all this awaited?
The hiss of scythe,
whirr of hone sharpening the blade,
and morning by morning, a thrush singing
from a favourite tree-top:
Get up, get!
Be quick, be quick, be quick!
Stick to it, stick to it!

Never now
shall I fear to surrender breath to Him
Who made these things —
marrying lightning's jagged jewel to thunder,
rapturous joy to pain,
bringing Life out of Death —
that beyond, clothed anew,
I may look again on my beloved,
with awed recognition!

[R.F.S.]